Business
Cyberbullies
and How to Fight Back

Business
Cyberbullies
and How to Fight Back

Debbie Elicksen

Self-Counsel Press
(a division of)
International Self-Counsel Press Ltd.
USA   Canada

Self-Counsel Press acknowledges the financial support of the Government of Canada through the Canada Book Fund (CBF) for our publishing activities.

Printed in Canada.

First edition: 2015

Library and Archives Canada Cataloguing in Publication

Elicksen, Debbie, author
    Business cyberbullies and how to fight back / Debbie Elicksen.

(Business series)
Issued in print and electronic formats.
ISBN 978-1-77040-220-1 (pbk.).—ISBN 978-1-77040-980-4 (epub).—
ISBN 978-1-77040-981-1 (kindle)

    1. Business enterprises—Computer networks—Security measures.
2. Computer security. 3. Data protection. I. Title. II. Series: Self-Counsel
business series

HF5548.37.E45 2015   658.4'78   C2014-908243-6
                                              C2014-908244-4

MIX
Paper from
responsible sources
FSC
www.fsc.org   FSC® C004071

Self-Counsel Press
(a division of)
International Self-Counsel Press Ltd.

Bellingham, WA   North Vancouver, BC
USA   Canada

Contents

Samples

Notice to Readers

Laws are constantly changing. Every effort is made to keep this publication as current as possible. However, the author, the publisher, and the vendor of this book make no representations or warranties regarding the outcome or the use to which the information in this book is put and are not assuming any liability for any claims, losses, or damages arising out of the use of this book. The reader should not rely on the author or the publisher of this book for any professional advice. Please be sure that you have the most recent edition.

Acknowledgments

This book would not have been possible if it were not for the personal guidance of Cynthia K. Seymour and Dianne Ojar-Ali. Robert Cairns, Donna Price, Donna Matheson, and Jennifer Miller-Bender also held my hand through the process.

Thank you to Dr. Michael Nuccitelli, Sara Hawkins, Annette Stanwick, Yngve Hauge, Thushyanthan Amirthelingam, Jeremy Pomeroy, Robert Cairns, Diane Ojar-Ali, and especially Jennifer Miller-Bender for being so gracious with their time in allowing me to interview them and use their material for this book.

A special shout-out to Coral Sterling, Rhonda Martin, Don and Molly Henderson, Stephen Bender, Blair Sveinson and my digital media disciples for their moral support.

Introduction

Cyberbullying is not just a schoolyard issue, but you would never know it when you type the word into a search engine.

I spent a lot of hours researching the Internet for cyberbullying resources that do not refer to students, schools, and parents. The amount of links that pertained to business cyberbullying could be counted on one hand.

In reality, when any adult, particularly a celebrity, politician, athlete, or corporate executive says something stupid (or nothing at all) the Internet social-sphere lights up with an onslaught of verbal assaults.

In nearly every YouTube and article comment feed, terrible untruths, language, and outright bullying behavior can be seen.

Workplace bullies follow employees home through the computer. Stalkers, ex-boyfriends/girlfriends seeking revenge, disgruntled job candidates that were passed over, creditors, or a stranger that dislikes the color of your eyes. Haters are everywhere and they are posting trash on the Internet.

Cyberbullying is not unlike identity theft — when there is a knowing and willful malicious act to discredit another person or business's reputation through a website or web post — that is an act of cyberbullying. It's happening in businesses all too often.

While there are crossovers between the classroom and the boardroom with respect to how cyberbullying comes about and how to deal with it, for the most part, the schoolyard doesn't impact a company's balance sheet. There are issues that only adults and businesses face and children do not. The effect on commerce and trade impacts the ability to do business. Collectively, it also hurts our economies.

Most of the cyberbullying statistics regard children. Business statistics are somewhat vague and tend to be more focused on offline workplace bullying and hacking. It is difficult to put an actual number on it, but the cases we know about are alarming.

A survey released by www.workplacebullying.org says that 65 million workers are affected nationwide (United States) by what could be considered workplace bullying. While it doesn't differentiate a virtual component, the lost production as a result of this is estimated at $180 million.

But an adult cyberbully doesn't have to be someone from your workspace. It could be your neighbor, your client, or your supplier. It could be someone you've never met.

Anyone can post anything on the Internet and in social networks, even libelous, hateful comments meant to destroy a person's credibility or business. Once it is out there, unless the owner of the site agrees, and without a court order, the likelihood is slim you can get the post removed. Then it comes down to whether you have the time and the money to spend months, maybe years, of energy and lawyers' visits to create a libel lawsuit and fight for your reputation.

Being a member of the Internet society means you get to experience the same venom you see with the likes of (name the celebrity). Knowing this should give you pause when you see a nasty post online in a Google search that is incongruent with the rest of the posts listed under a person's name or from what you personally know about him or her. The next time the post could be about you and there doesn't have to be a reason.

None of us is immune.

Internet thought leader and author of the book *What Happens in Vegas Stays on YouTube* Erik Qualman says it is all right if there are a couple

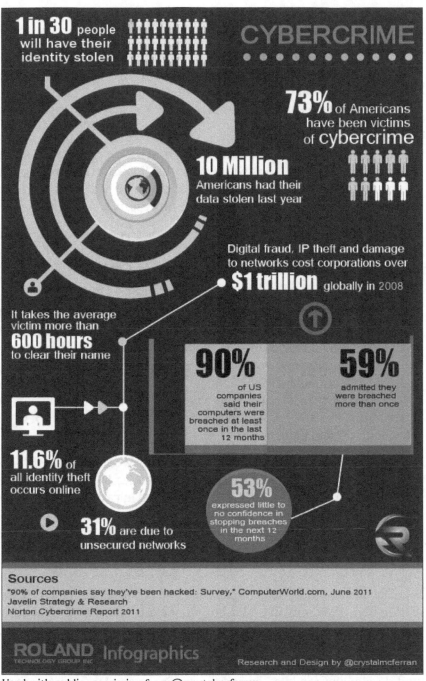

1 in 30 people will have their identity stolen

CYBERCRIME

73% of Americans have been victims of cybercrime

10 Million Americans had their data stolen last year

Digital fraud, IP theft and damage to networks cost corporations over **$1 trillion** globally in 2008

It takes the average victim more than **600 hours** to clear their name

90% of US companies said their computers were breached at least once in the last 12 months

59% admitted they were breached more than once

11.6% of all identity theft occurs online

53% expressed little to no confidence in stopping breaches in the next 12 months

31% are due to unsecured networks

Sources
"90% of companies say they've been hacked: Survey," ComputerWorld.com, June 2011
Javelin Strategy & Research
Norton Cybercrime Report 2011

ROLAND Infographics
TECHNOLOGY GROUP INC
Research and Design by @crystalmcferran

Used with public permission from @crystalmcferran

of ugly posts out there about you. It means you are human or that humans run your business. However, that still doesn't make it any easier for you when you discover a cyberslur that completely ruins your world.

If you find yourself the target at the end of somebody's keyboard, there are stages you will go through. There is no sugar-coating it. You will be hit emotionally. It will be devastating. You may even lose friends over it.

There are lessons to be learned from other people's pain, and I hope to share these lessons with you in this book. This includes a list of dos and don'ts. You will need a plan and time to heal. The intention of this book is to guide you through the process.

The first thing you need to know is that you are not alone. It doesn't matter what your profession is. When you face the wrath of a keystroke, you, your business, the nation's most polarizing politician, and the celebrity of the week are in the same sorority.

Jennifer Miller-Bender's story is a perfect introduction to round off this point. She fits the gamut - adult, business, and celebrity wrapped in one. You can feel the emotional stages she experienced through her story. You can see how some of her mistakes (engaging the bullies) factored into her bullies' behaviors. As you follow her journey, you can also see the story resolve with the ultimate lesson: we can only remain true to ourselves and not let others dictate our fate, regardless of what they do to try and influence us.

Jennifer Miller-Bender got her start in Hollywood casting with Executive Producer Al Burton on the sets of Charles in Charge and The New Lassie. In the early 1990s, Jennifer worked in casting and with the Matthau Company. Besides casting, she was a talent scout, in management, and raised funds for films. In the late 1990s, she acquired a lease from DreamWorks for the 22nd floor of the Universal Building, where her company JMCasting was housed until 2003.

She owned Model Search Magazine and scouted talent all over the nation from 1988 until 2000 for both modeling and as an early casting tool. From 2003 to 2008, she went to MTSC Productions in Las Vegas, where she cast and co-produced, as well as acquired sponsors, product placement, and advertising for the USA World Showcase. She found and developed Grandma Lee and the singing superstar from America's Got Talent: Jackie Evancho.

Jennifer has worked with all the major studios, including Universal, Warner Brothers, FOX, Disney, and Paramount. She worked with Bill Dance Casting, Central Casting, Aaron Spelling, Al Burton, Ron Howard, Frank Darabont, Scott Mednick, Dennis Quaid, Walter Matthau, Charlie Matthau, Jack Lemmon, Sissy Spacek, Kevin Kline, and many more.

When Jennifer met her husband, she left Los Angeles and moved with him to Arizona. They commuted back and forth from Phoenix to California about three weeks each month so she could continue her work in entertainment.

She raised her kids in Arizona many years prior, and back then, that state was considered one of the top three places in the US to film movies. Since then, it had dropped to the bottom. So naturally, she wanted to help bring the movie industry back to the area.

Jennifer reconnected with Sean Kapera (who photographed her in the early 1990s and 2000s at red carpet events, sets, and casting calls). She had actually started his career. Sean took her to a local film industry meeting, where he was a board member.

"I now realize they were hobbyists trying to do independent film. But then I thought, this was better than anywhere to start. The new Screen Actors Guild (SAG) president for Arizona was going to be speaking. I had dealt with SAG and understood it. When I spoke to them about bringing in real movies, I didn't realize I was stepping on toes."

Some of the local industry people were working on getting credits for Internet Movie Database (IMDb), a resume site for film industry people. They sought producing credits by doing short films that were only distributed locally. The local film group included a clique of individuals who Jennifer wasn't familiar with, as none of them were around when Jennifer was last in the city.

When Jennifer said it was about time Arizona took back the film industry it used to have, she didn't realize that actually scared these people. Jennifer had the ability to not only get everybody SAG unionized, which would allow them to do SAG films (and get paid more), but it would also open the doors to bring in SAG films, which meant Diane Keaton, Dennis Quaid, or another A-lister Jennifer had worked with before. But that also meant the SAG A-lister would then take the principal role in a film production and it would ultimately leave out the people who weren't union.

However, Jennifer didn't see it that way. She saw it as, "Now we'll have five movies here that made $100 million and brought revenue to Arizona."

What ended up being another red flag to the local film people was the fact that Jennifer wasn't listed on IMDb. But to people in Hollywood, she could just say she was Walter's (Matthau) girl or that she worked with Jack Lemmon, Al Burton, Aaron Spelling, or Steven Spielberg. She didn't need to be on IMDb.

The reason she wasn't on IMDb was due to a simple mistake made by an administrator.

"I was doing projects before IMDb even existed. I had a lot of stalkers when I was on the 22nd floor of Universal. In order to be CSA (Casting Society of America) accredited and be on IMDb when it first started, you had to go through a process. The assistant, who is now a casting director, and by the way I'm very proud of, made a simple mistake and put my home address and phone number on one of the application lines. Because I had restraining orders on a few people that were crazy, I took myself off IMDb and was a big activist against it. So my being on IMDb wasn't ever going to happen. I didn't need it. I was going through a divorce, too, so I was working with a well-known casting agency but as an independent contractor so that I could make a living. They knew darn well who my ex-husband was and how controlling he was. I've done many newspaper articles about it, so it's not a secret. Everybody knew [he] controlled me and was out to get me."

Jennifer used to travel and scout to bring in pretty people who were just getting started. They would get the day rate, and even though they were non-union, because they were pretty (men and women), they would get $695 instead of $100. After a while, each actor could make enough money to pay for their SAG dues and become union. That meant they could take one- to five-liners (have a few sentences in a movie). The more lines an actor has means the more money he or she gets. Jennifer could set it up where actors could come in for two to three weeks into California, get their feet wet, rent a monthly motel with a kitchenette, and see if their careers were going to go further. In the meantime, she replaced the talent that didn't make it with more pretty people. They used to call her the Queen of Extras.

As long as the casting agency brought Jennifer movies, she didn't care about how much she was getting paid due to the non-compete clause her ex-husband made her sign.

So back in Phoenix, her plan was to take a busload of people from Arizona to California and get them SAG unionized at the casting agency. She had it all set up, and arranged that they could appear on the television show *Entourage* because she knew someone and had worked on it before.

"I was making deals with the casting agency and said something like, hey, I'll let you cast with me this Will Smith movie if you bring my people into *Entourage* and give them SAG vouchers. So I pissed off a group of people in Hollywood who thought I was taking their money because the casting agency could pay me less, and I pissed off a group of people in Arizona. Both of those groups combined together and went after me."

One of those disgruntled Hollywood casting directors was on payroll with the casting agency when he worked with Jennifer on a movie. He had anger issues and came to the set and threatened an actress with a hunting knife. He was removed from the set and knew Jennifer had signed the protection document the casting agency had everyone sign.

The combined group started three or four Facebook pages, named things such as "I Hate Jennifer Miller" or "I'm Jennifer Miller and I Am a Fraud". They used the sites to discredit her and deny her background in entertainment.

"Facebook did not help at all. I wrote them. I got attorneys. I paid thousands of dollars to get the site down. It wasn't me, and they were taking my pictures and defacing them. There were pictures from the Emmys."

She tried desperately to justify her career with the local clique. "I was showing people Emmy tickets and they were telling me that I was an usher. If they really knew anything about ushers at the Emmys, they stand in back of the red ropes and they're in black only. I was in the prettiest pink dress and it was in every fashion police entertainment magazine. I pulled out the magazines to show them. They said I Photoshopped them. I said you can go in the archives. I brought them into my home to see my memorabilia. Then they went back on that site and said I was a fraud — because I scared them."

They were not going to stop. Jennifer surmised it was because there were two general emotions at play: fear and love. Her passion was to bring all this to fruition, to put Phoenix and Arizona back on the Hollywood map (love), and they were too afraid. So she took a step back, took down all of her profiles, but decided to leave her real Facebook pages up, despite her lawyer's advice to take them down. No matter what they wrote, she would post positive things on Facebook. "Today is good. I woke up. I'm still living. My life is wonderful."

Meanwhile, Jennifer connected with Charlie Matthau, then Scott Mednick, Dennis Quaid, and others, and played it low key while working on film funding.

She did seem to have the perfect life. She had the husband who adored her and she adored him. They were making money. They were attending Emmys and Oscars, talking to producers, and she was back with Matthau and Mednick, doing charity things, and working with Eva Longoria, Diane Keaton, and others.

The knife-wielding fellow then took the cyberbullying to an offline level and Jennifer's private investigator confirmed that he looked to be in pursuit her family, too.

Jennifer confirmed, "I had the police drive by all the time. They were on alert. It got really dirty. He (the knife-wielding casting agent) said (in a public Facebook post) he would treat me like a wounded deer during hunting season and that he would skin me alive and then dice me up into little pieces and eat me. I had bodyguards from Navy SEALs out of Portland that went on that website confirming this."

"Here's the thing, this was a Facebook fan page. So they would ask you to like it. People would like it, like my stepson and others, thinking it was for me. They weren't reading it, they just liked it. Also at that time, I had a casting page on Facebook. Overnight it had 5,000 followers within less than 24 hours. That's how popular I was and it scared everybody. Oh, she's coming back, and our little trickle stuff, she's going to take money from us now. She's going to go to these seminars and tell people about casting and no one is going to listen to us anymore — and she's only charging $75 and we charge $1,000. I wasn't intentionally doing it. They saw that I was hurting their pocketbook. I was just trying to get something done."

The bullies' Facebook pages finally disappeared. Then Diane Keaton came to her rescue by seeing one of the California casting directors to tell him, "You don't know who you're messing with. She's real. Leave her alone."

They started backing off. Then other industry people would go to her Facebook personal site and write, great seeing you again. Remember the old days with Walter?

Jennifer then said to heck with it and accepted the fact they were going to attack her. Her husband was still nervous about it because some of them had threatened her physically. When her old bodyguard told her she needed to get a gun, then they knew it was real. When a guy says he's going to gut you and slice and dice you, on a public forum, and the rest of the bullies feed off it, that is when cyberbullying turns into a real-life physical threat.

"In the end, I just stood true. I knew who I was. My husband knew who I was. One of the most proudest days — and I bawled like a baby — I sat there with Sean Kapera from the old days, who I wasn't supposed to see because of my ex-husband's non-compete clause. But since my ex-husband had passed, all these people were my connection back into the industry. I didn't have to honor the non-compete clause anymore. So here's Sean Kapera on one side, me, my husband across the table, and Charlie Matthau, and we're talking about Walter [Matthau], and Jack [Lemmon] — granted they passed, but all the good times. There was a twinkle in my eye and Charlie turned to me and Sean turned to me at the same time. My husband recognized the twinkle as happiness. At the same time, these two guys that I worked with saw that the passion was back. Here I was with the new man in my life with the old men in my life, reliving, and growing this, making it bigger, working on another project again in the middle of the place where it started. I just started tearing up and bawling. I knew the others didn't matter anymore. The minute they didn't matter anymore is the minute I took back me."

Then Jennifer had the challenge of recreating herself. Although Jen Miller was her name, it was also a persona. It was a patented name. Jen Miller was an entity as much as the name was her. Jen Miller was JM Casting, Universal, and all the things she had done under this name.

Meanwhile, she and Stephen got involved raising money for a charity that provided money to get kids into acting. Jennifer arranged for Paul Walker to be at an event. When Walker didn't show up, it added fuel to the cyberbullies' fire. Unfortunately, while Walker knew Jennifer had changed her last name to Bender, he forgot to tell his publicist and the event organizer used the name Jennifer Bender. Everyone in Hollywood knew her as Jen Miller.

Making that connection between her persona and her married name took some time. Today, whether you look for Jennifer Miller or Jennifer Bender, you can find the same person. As of a couple of years ago, all of the cyberbullying posts had disappeared.

"There were a lot of people who hated people who were happy," Jennifer admits. "They had to make my world terrible and I let them for a while. All these people I knew from Hollywood would tell these people — and they were nobodies — who I was and they still they wouldn't believe it. I kept trying to justify myself. No matter what I did, there was never a situation I could have fixed, where I could have given them the right answer."

This book is for everyone who has felt the pain of an ugly post, who has had their identity compromised in some way, who has been bullied digitally. Don't cancel your Twitter and Facebook accounts. Don't start using a new email address. You don't owe your bully anything, especially your digital life or your physical life. Instead, learn how to regain your identity by making the bully an insignificant blob on your road to personal enrichment. This book will show you how to take control of your digital footprint, how to create Internet content that is on your terms, and how to disengage your "haters."

> *If you're horrible to me, I'm going to write a song about it, and you won't like it. That's how I operate.*
>
> — TAYLOR SWIFT

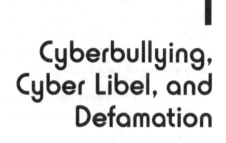

1

Cyberbullying, Cyber Libel, and Defamation

A lie can travel halfway around the world while the truth is putting on its shoes.

— Mark Twain

Cyberspace is an abstract, artificial electronic universe. In reality, it is an illusion. However, we treat it like it is an entity and it consumes our world. If you want to test out this theory, try leaving your smartphone untouched in a drawer for a day and disengage from the web completely.

According to Dr. Michael Nuccitelli, a New York psychologist, the Internet, or information technology, directly influences a child's identity formation. But as an adult reading this text, you know inside of your being that it directly influences your identity formation, too.

Everything we do and touch is tied to the Internet. When you register your car, when a child is born, and every retail purchase you make goes into a digital database that is hooked up to an Internet cloud that can be accessed from another location. Your banking, bill payments, and even your taxes are accessed online. Even if your life is lived solely offline (no website, email, online memberships, or social media), your digital footprint is automatic whenever you apply for a job, a credit card, or a newspaper delivery or get arrested.

Think about it. Our whole purpose for marketing our business is so that people will find us. The Internet is our number one tool. Search Engine Optimization is the buzz to which all of our business branding is based on.

The Internet has offered up a lot of great things. This is where innovation happens, where we can connect with people across the globe without leaving our computer screen. This is more than a tool for us now. It is our lifestyle. How long can you go in a day without checking your emails or Facebook?

The Internet is not just a playground where kids hang out. It is our livelihood, our resume, our main communications tool.

We hear a lot about cyberbullying in the classroom, and if you research the term, one can easily think it is only an issue that faces children.

Children grow up. They get jobs and move into the workplace. Before that happens, many of them take their cues from adult behavior. The Internet is where they are most comfortable. It's where their friends live.

The same is true for adults. It's where our friends and business connections are.

Bill Belsey, Keewatin Divisional Board of Education (KDBE) and the Government of the Northwest Territories and founder of bullying.org, said: "Cyberbullying involves the use of information and communication technologies to support deliberate, repeated, and hostile behavior by an individual or group, that is intended to harm others."

When you think of cyberbullying, don't think of it as just a schoolyard issue. You don't have to go too far to find someone you know who has been affected. You see it every day. You just haven't recognized it as cyberbullying.

A physical bully is known and can see his or her target's reaction. Cyberbullying is when bullying behavior goes online.

Sometimes WE are the cyberbullies and we don't know it. We may perpetuate this behavior when our intentions are to warn others of a potential fraud, or we just want to overshare our opinion in a social media post. I've done it, and I've had it happen to me, both knowingly and unintentionally.

We may all be cybercriminals, intentionally or unintentionally. Let's change that here and now. If you recognize yourself doing any of the adverse behaviors you read about in this book, and you are scared, appalled, and don't want to hurt anyone, now you know.

Sometimes a post or comment, even if it is mean, won't rattle the target or give them pause. They may just chalk it up to moronism. But there are others who take the comments so personally, it acts like a knife in their hearts, and their psyche can be so fragile already that they may consider drastic measures as a result of it. Adults commit suicide, too, but they also can turn to violent payback.

1. When Does Digital Content Cross the Line?

In a nutshell, these are all forms of digital content infractions:

1. When false information is spread about someone with intent to harm his or her reputation.

2. When a person is singled out and attacked or made fun of.

3. When an account is hijacked and false information is spread about the person whose account was compromised.

4. When images or private files are shared publicly with the intent to embarrass a person or harm his or her reputation.

5. When someone is excluded or shunned from a group.

6. When ugly, toxic, and hateful comments are repeatedly sent to harass someone.

While all of the above apply, legally, much of adult cyberbullying falls under these legal categories:

- Slander.

- Libel.

- Defamation.

- Harassment.

1.1 Slander

Slander is the equivalent to conversations behind someone's back like in the movie Mean Girls. Slander pertains more to the spoken word, even if it appears in a transcribed text from audio or video.

If a detrimental opinion is verbalized about someone, it does not always make it slanderous. Sometimes whether something is slander will depend on the context.

It is slanderous if someone accuses you of a crime outside of telling it to law enforcement. It is slanderous to say you have a contagious disease, that you're adulterous, or to verbally drag your business through the mud.

For example, if someone says verbally that John has two sets of company books, implying he gives the illegal set to the taxman, unless there is proof and if John has not been charged with any crime, this would be a slanderous statement. But if a legal investigation had discovered this to be true, then it is a truthful statement, even if it was said as an opinion. If true, it would not qualify as slander.

A slanderous statement, as it is spoken out loud, may not be on record as having been said, so the target would have to prove he or she suffered a financial loss in order to collect damages.

YourDictionary.com as of November, 2014 offers these as slander examples, and more:

- "New Zealanders who emigrate to Australia raise the IQs of both countries." — a quote from New Zealand Prime Minister Rob Muldoon. The implication is that New Zealand is glad to see these people leave and that Australia is lucky to get them.

- Joe Francis, founder of *Girls Gone Wild* said casino mogul Steve Wynn threatened to kill him because of a gambling debt. Wynn was awarded a $19-million judgment that was upheld in an appellate court. A jury awarded Wynn $40 million that a judge later shaved down[1].

Slander only qualifies for a lawsuit if the statement is false and has done serious harm.

---

1 "Verdict upheld against 'Girls Gone Wild' founder in spat with Steve Wynn," LasVegasSun.com, accessed November, 2014. www.lasvegassun.com/news/2014/jun/23/verdict-upheld-against-girls-gone-wild-founder

1.2 Libel

Statements that are published in printed or electronic format, such as in blog posts, articles, any other form of printed media, chat room conversations, and online comments can be considered libel if the content is inflammatory and untrue.

If the source is radicalized and known to spout malicious charges about a person or business, it may not be libel if the audience doesn't consider it a slur. The Pew Research Center cites Fox News as an example of an organization that is known to skew facts[2]. There have been some successful libel suits against the media giant, but there are just as many dropped[3], and probably more that are not filed[4].

Comments that qualify as libel leave a permanent record because printed material lasts and anything published online at one time can always be retrieved. But the person who made the post will win on defense if the content is true, if the person acted in good faith and without malice, or the comment was a statement of opinion based on fact and without malice.

When content purposely shames, disgraces, ridicules, or intentionally injures someone's reputation or occupation, it is considered libel when the accusations are false.

Well-known entertainment figures and public figures have been the brunt of numerous libelous comments, and it isn't that easy for celebrities to win libel lawsuits.

A private individual doesn't have to prove the same actual malice that someone in the public eye might; content that is published knowing it was false or "with reckless disregard of whether it was false or not." (United States tort law) Actual malice is a legal definition you will only see in the United States.

1.3 Defamation

Both slander and libel fall under defamation. The circulation of false information that has the potential to damage a reputation is what defamation of character is all about.

---

2 "5 facts about Fox News," PewResearch.org, accessed November, 2014. www.pewresearch.org/fact-tank/ 2014/01/14/five-facts-about-fox-news
3 "Fox TV Can't Escape $28 Million Defamation Lawsuit Brought by Judge," HollywoodReporter.com, accessed November, 2014. www.hollywoodreporter.com/thr-esq/fox-tv-cant-escape-28-382874
4 "Why Limbaugh or Fox News Are Never Sued for Libel," DailyKos.com, accessed November, 2014. www.dailykos.com/story/2007/01/09/288674/-Why-Limbaugh-or-Fox-News-Are-Never-Sued-for-Libel#

Web defamation is a cheap way for an ungratified client, an ex-boyfriend, an adversary, or someone looking to air dirty laundry can get back at someone. It doesn't matter what poisonous words are created, it is a purposeful act meant to erode someone's character.

Bullying behavior is meant to be hurtful. It is intended to disparage someone's character, and to threaten, embarrass, or intimidate the person. Bullying behavior leads to slanderous and libelous statements that are perpetuated in a harassing manner.

Yngve Hauge is from Molde, Norway and has implemented an event called We Walk Together Against Bullying (showrespect.wordpress.com) where he treks across the country and speaks to people about bullying along the way. This is how he personally has exorcised the effects of his own encounters with bullies.

"It's a problem with insecurity," Hauge spoke in a live interview on Virtual Newsmakers. "To make themselves more secure, they have to make themselves bigger than they are. Someone might speak differently; new children at the beginning of school, maybe you're quiet and don't talk as much. It's very easy to start bullying. Most people don't know how much damage they do."

Whether the bully is known or anonymous, he or she doesn't always see the consequences of any post. Unless the target responds directly, there is no visual feedback.

We hear the term "Internet troll" mixed in with cyberbullying. While trolls do conduct a form of cyberbullying, they do have different intents.

Trulioo.com's blog[5] describes the variances in simple terms.

Cyberbullies:

- Intent is to harm.

- Resentful and seeking revenge.

- Shows authority.

- You may know who they are.

Trolls:

- Intent is to upset.

---

5   "What's the difference between a Cyber Bully and a Cyber Troll? And, Tips on How to Handle Cyber Bullies and Trolls," Trulioo.com, accessed November, 2014. www.trulioo.com/blog/2013/07/23/is-there-a-difference-between-cyberbullies-and-cyber-trolls

- Seeking attention or recognition.
- Vent and disrupt.
- They like to be anonymous.

Here are some courses of action when dealing with these types.

Cyberbullies:

- Ignore them, do not respond.
- Document their actions, and use screenshots.
- Block them everywhere on all networks.
- Report their activity to social networks, ISPs, and where appropriate.

Trolls:

- Know they exist and expect to encounter them.
- Ignore them since they feed on engagement.
- Report them to moderators and administrators.
- Use verification tools on your website.

2
The Psychology of a Cyberbully

Bullying is a national epidemic.

— MACKLEMORE

Dr. Michael Nuccitelli is a New York state licensed psychologist and certified forensic consultant with a doctoral degree in clinical psychology. He is a cyberbullying, Internet safety, cybercrime, online predator, and forensic psychology educator and investigator. He founded iPredator Inc. (www.ipredator.co) in 2011 to provide a public resource to help reduce victimization from online assailants.

Whether the perpetrator has committed an act of cyberbullying, cyber libel, Internet trolling, or any other similar adverse behavior, Dr. Nuccitelli calls them all the same thing: an iPredator.

On his website, he describes the iPredator as "a person, group, or nation who, directly or indirectly, engages in exploitation, victimization, coercion, stalking, theft or disparagement of others using Information and Communications Technology. iPredators are driven by deviant fantasies, desires for power and control, retribution, religious fanaticism, political reprisal, psychiatric illness, perceptual distortions, peer acceptance or personal financial gain. iPredators can be any age or gender and are not bound by economic status, race, religion, or national heritage." (November, 2014.)

An adult assailant has already, theoretically, developmentally matured and reached his or her formative milestones. The iPredator does not bully another adult to feel machismo or marianismo. He or she is driven by a strong need for power and control, whereas a child bully's motive is more about peer acceptance and recognition.

A bully offender usually knows the target. The assailant benefits from what he or she is doing to the target. They might have had a past relationship.

"This is where we talk about adult bullying and where the lines kind of get murky," adds Nuccitelli, "because it is also cyber harassment. To me, it's all the same. It's online nonsense."

The doctor warns, "The one thing you want to be careful of is the use of the term psychopath. Be mindful of how you use it. The psychopath has no guilt or shame. Your vast majority of adult bullies, they are fuelled by the target's engagement, whereas a true psychopath, you can jump through hoops and backwards, he is not affected by your reaction. He'll change his strategies and he still may find joy in seeing you go crazy. But he has no affect."

According to Nuccitelli, iPredopaths (online psychopaths) are not known to break the law. They can be grandiose, are habitually deceptive, and have a much higher rate of engaging in violent, sadistic, and severely depraved behaviors than the general population. They are not necessarily homicidal, sexually perverted, or overtly violent and are highly functioning, thus capable of being part of the political, religious, and corporate elite. They can also be community leaders.

The veil of anonymity of cyberspace is unlocking the proverbial Pandora's box in all of us. We can be anyone we want to be and hide stealth in the background to watch those around us.

Dr. Nuccitelli believes all criminal deviant psychopathology — all of it — has to be re-profiled. "We grew up without information technology. Then now we are enveloped by it. We are going to see how it envelopes us even more. It is just so embarrassing to have my field of psychologists that literally do not take into consideration the information age."

When he first wrote iPredator and took the concept to his peers, they told him the basis of his foundation was incorrect, because they figured only the criminally deviant and the violently disturbed used information technology as tools for bullying. They did not take into account that cyberspace was a new dimension.

On the Internet, your size, muscles, and strength have nothing to do with your venom. Passive aggression is the subtlety of communication. It is the capacity to use the spoken and written word. Both genders can excel at it.

This is the first time we are engaging in interpersonal exchanges without using our five senses. The purpose of our five senses is self-preservation, procreation, and to carry on the species. In cyberspace, that's all lost.

What is left is the individual's interpretation of what he or she is seeing and reading. What might be a pleasing, stimulating conversation to one person, may be a personal affront to another. The words are the same. What's different is the interpretation. There is no vocal inflection to interpret. Everything is left to the brain and the mind to try and extrapolate and make sense of.

Dr. Nuccitelli agrees that recognized individuals are not getting very good advice on how to deal with cyberbullying (which we will address later in the book). Those who bully, harass, and stalk celebrities — part of their condition is that they want to be accepted and recognized. "Whether someone is psychotic, psychopathic, or just [a jerk], they have a strong need to be a part of the high profile person's journey. They want to ride the coattails of that celebrity. There's also a payoff to the knockdown. For celebrities, public figures, and those that are in the spotlight, they have the same themes as any person or business going through this, but they sometimes have different circumstances."

Victims may not be Charlize Theron, but could be the mayor of some small town in Wisconsin, the pastor of a church, or a well-known corporate leader. Anybody who is a public figure or a leading figure recognized among the social pack has a much higher rate of being targeted. The iPredator is looking for power and control, so they will go after someone who is already there in their eyes.

We know that for the recognized figure to say something back, then it makes them look like the bad guy. The iPredator wants to provoke the target to the point where he or she gets a reaction.

Then there are stalkers of cyber stars that are intimacy seekers. But non-famous people can have a similar experience. Stalkers are everywhere. It's just a matter of who they decide to target next. They could choose their next victim based on their Facebook picture or their Twitter profile.

In some instances, bullies might exhibit antisocial behavior. Some may have committed other crimes. They could be addicted to substances and have poor academic skills[1]. The bottom line is a bully is angry. They could be upset with the target and want to make that person feel as much pain as they are feeling. They could be mad at the world and have sought out the first person who has crossed their path.

1. What Cyberbullies Do

Brian Martin is the international director of Whistleblowers Australia and works at Wollongong University. In the February 2006 edition of The Whistle, a newsletter of Whistleblowers Australia, he described five commonly used methods that bullies use[2].

1. Cover up the deed. They are nice to your face but talk trash behind your back.

2. Denigrate the target. The intention is to discredit. If the target tries to fight or argue back, the bully uses that against them and as proof of why their action was necessary.

3. Reinterpret what happened. They could be retelling hearsay and deny their intent to malign. Then they might laugh it off and tell others they were just kidding.

4. Use official channels to give the appearance of justice.

5. Intimidate opponents. The bully will threaten reprisal if the target tries to fight back.

1.1 Types of actions that bullies take

Internet revenge comes in all sorts of forms. Here are three common angles that some targets might experience:

---

1 "Bullying," ChildTrends.org, accessed November, 2014. www.childtrends.org/?indicators=bullying#sthash.6qVgX0Qh.dpuf
2 "What to do when you've been defamed," Brian Martin, accessed November, 2014. www.bmartin.cc/pubs/06whistle.html

- Being accused of a scam.

- Being accused of being a rip-off.

- Being accused of being a fraud.

The bully will wield his or her message using everything available, especially where the target is located, such as on certain social media platforms. He or she will focus on keywords to ensure that whenever someone Googles the target's name, their ugly posts will show up.

The bully might threaten the target physically, with hostile teasing, prey on the target's emotional stability, and engage in outright harassment.

There are 38 cyberbullying tactics that have been categorized by Dr. Nuccitelli. While the list was initially compiled regarding child iPredators, these are exact behaviors that are done by adults. He adds, "Children are far more advanced in social media and information technology. Adults are just mimicking what kids are doing to each other."

The online bully is "a person, group, or nation who directly or indirectly engages in exploitation, victimization, coercion, stalking, theft, or disparagement of others using information and communications technology."

Predators are driven by deviant fantasy, power and control, retribution, religious fanaticism, political reprisal, psychiatric illness, distorted perceptions, peer acceptance, or personal and financial gain. They can be any age, any gender, economic status, race, religion, or heritage.

1.2 Cyberbullying tactics

Here is the list of tactics Dr. Nuccitelli discusses:

1. Exclusion: The iPredator targets a person's need to feel accepted and be part of the social construct.

2. Flaming: An online passionate argument that frequently includes profane and vulgar language in a public environment, such as discussion boards, groups, and chat rooms.

3. Exposure: A public display, posting or forwarding of sensitive or sexual personal communication, images or video.

4. eIntimidation: The iPredator wants to inspire fear by communicating threats. The fear can be implied or direct.

5. Cyber harassment: The assailant sends hurtful, frequent, and serious messages worded in a severe, persistent, and pervasive manner that is negative and frequent.

6. Phishing: A cyber attack to trick, persuade, or manipulate someone into revealing personal or financial information.

7. Impersonation: The iPredator will make unpopular comments in the target's name or set up websites with vitriolic information.

8. Denigration: The assailant sends, posts, publishes cruel rumors, gossip, and untrue statements in order to humiliate and disparage the target.

9. Mobile device image sharing: Pornographic or graphic pictures are sent to everyone in the address book.

10. Image/video dissemination: Nonconsensual images and/or videos are emailed to peers or published on websites to humiliate or disparage the target.

11. Interactive gaming harassment: The bully uses verbal abuse, threatening and profane language, locks others out of games, passes false information about others, and hacks into accounts.

12. Porn and marketing list insertion: The iPredator signs the target up to numerous junk marketing or pornographic sites for emails and instant message lists. A target can receive hundreds, even thousands of messages a day.

13. Cyberstalking: This can be the most dangerous of cyberbullying tactics. It will include threats of harm, intimidation, and offensive comments but with the threat or belief of an offline threat.

14. Griefing: The cyberbully habitually and chronically causes frustration by not following rules of an interactive online video game, and intentionally disrupts the immersion of another player in their gameplay.

15. Password theft and lockout: The iPredator steals a password and pretends to be the target.

16. Web page assassination: The assailant creates websites that insult or endanger someone.

17. Voting and polling booth degradation: In existing online polling/voting sites or a newly created website, a poll will be posted to

allow others to vote for categories that will be highly embarrassing and depreciating to the target. The iPredator encourages groups to disparage a target.

18. Bash boards: Negative and depreciating information is posted in online bulletin boards.

19. Hoodwinking: This is similar to phishing where the target is tricked to divulge information, which then gets published in a negative way, rather than the way that was expected when the perpetrator sought for the information.

20. Happy slapping: This integrates video and bullying, where the target is attacked or embarrassed in person. The moment is videotaped and then spread virally online.

21. Text wars and attacks: The bully and accomplices gang up on the target by sending hundreds of emails and texts.

22. Malicious code dissemination: A malicious code (via virus, spyware or hacking program) is sent to the target disguised in a link, photograph, video in order to damage or harm the target's information technology communications.

23. Warning wars: False allegations are sent to the target's ISP about their posting inappropriate information — often enough to get the target's account suspended.

24. Screen name mirroring: The iPredator constructs a screen name similar to the target's so as to appear as the target.

25. Cyber drama: This is gossip that was not to be shared on a blog or flame war and it ends after a few messages — likely because the target was able to block it. This is a passive aggressive form of cyberbullying.

26. Sexting: The iPredator distributes images or videos that are sexually explicit in nature or a sex-themed message or image.

27. Pseudonym stealth: The perpetrator is online when they might appear offline. Their identity is secret when they use messaging services. This could be done through a fake account.

28. Instant message attacks: The iPredator uses instant messages to send harassing and threatening messages.

29. Cyberbullying by proxy: The assailant encourages or persuades others to engage in depreciating and harassing the target.

30. Social media cyberbullying: The assailant will contact the target's friends or buddy lists to disseminate disparaging information.

31. Digital piracy inclusion: The iPredator encourages the target to engage in digital piracy, such as illegal reproduction and distribution of copyrighted material, then he or she reports it to authorities.

32. Tragedy news mirroring: The assailant threatens a target that they will plan and engage in a violent activity directed at their school or community.

33. Slut shaming: Images and videos of the target that can be construed as sexually provocative are recorded and published to induce shame.

34. Cyber threats: This is a passive aggressive strategy of provoking fear by informing the target he or she is in danger from an unknown assailant.

35. Trolling: The cyberbully disparages and harasses unidentified online users but may still know the identity of the target.

36. Sextortion: A target is exploited for sex or sexually themed activities in exchange for not disclosing information that is embarrassing or humiliating.

37. Twitter pooping: The cyberbully uses tweets to disparage and humiliate the target.

38. Micro-visual cyberbullying: A Vine-like clip (a short video) is sent to traumatize the target.

3
Who Is Most at Risk?

Anyone with an Internet account is technically at risk of a cyberattack, even if his or her only participation on the web is to use email.

Dianne Ojar-Ali is the author of Mrs. Fraud and You[1] and is the first Canadian member of the Identity Theft Professional Association. She sees that most people are at risk for cyber fraud and bullying. It isn't simply that you can go about your own business, mind your Ps and Qs and everything will be all right. When it happens it is a big deal.

"People don't realize how devastating a situation can be until we talk about it. They're very naïve. It's selfish in a way, too. They're not willing to learn anything about themselves holistically even though their business is about networking."

A part of your business plan should include protecting yourself, both as a business and individually, making yourself cyberbully-aware.

"We don't think of ourselves as we should," Ojar-Ali characterizes. "We're precious. We have to protect our fingerprint."

Your fingerprint includes your social security/social insurance number and you do not have to share it with anyone, even when applying

---

1   MrsFraudandYou.com, accessed November, 2014. http://mrsfraudandyou.com

for a job. The only time a potential employer will need it is if they hire you. Until then, why do they need it? Are they planning to do a full credit check without your permission?

Ojar-Ali adds that no one should be asking your date of birth, nor do they need the year you graduated. While it may be difficult getting around the date of birth issue while setting up a social media profile, adding your graduation year is usually optional. People do not need to know your age, especially a potential employer before you are hired.

We might do everything to the book and are the perfect digital citizen. It doesn't minimize your risk of being cyberbullied.

"Anything can happen at any point in time," explains Ojar-Ali. "An office romance ends with the possibility of it coming back to haunt you. People do things because of jealousy or because they have something to prove. People also love to gossip."

When you are a target of a bully, it really has more to do about the bully than you or anything you've done. You can attribute the following observations to most cyberbullies and Internet trolls:

- We don't believe in people because we don't believe in us.

- We don't love others because we don't love ourselves.

- We don't offer confidence in others because we don't have confidence in ourselves.

- Whatever we lack, we lash out for in other people.

- What we lack is what we project.

People are social pack animals, according to Dr. Michael Nuccitelli. "In every social construct, and it doesn't matter what you subscribe to, there are always those in a hierarchy that are weaker. The weak link is always the first to be targeted. We can no longer assume that the assailant is a male going after a female. Because females are taking more leadership roles, the psychological dynamics within a system, women are becoming assailants, particularly in the workplace."

Whether a person is the target of one or more adult cyberbullies or cyberbullying by proxy, the result is the same. The target feels isolated. The target feels as if he or she has no recourse and that there is nowhere to turn.

Depending on psychological makeup, constitution, and resilience, if the person is fragile, if they're going through a personal trauma, or having financial problems, he or she may feel the pressure of a cyberbullying attack more than someone with healthier self-esteem.

If one's offline world is stressful, painful, and emotional to where self-esteem is diminished, when the person goes onto the web, he or she may be looking for recognition and acceptance — to be heard. The person is more likely to engage in behavior that ignores Internet safety, but also to engage in high-risk online activities.

Home, school, work, finances, and other offline factors can cause significant distress. So with that, regardless of age, a person is more apt to be less vigilant when it comes to Internet safety and engage in risky online behavior.

Dr. Nuccitelli advises there are two words when it comes to adult bullying: personal information. With that, there are three ways one can interact with information:

1. Compiling.

2. Dissemination.

3. Exchange.

"There is nothing wrong with compiling. It's when we disseminate and exchange when life turns to hell. Personal information is the Achilles heel for all of us. The personal information you put out in cyberspace is permanent. It's not something that fades away. It doesn't just get deleted because somebody isn't talking about it."

Unsuspecting, vulnerable, submissive, unprepared businesses and psychologically distressed adults are at higher risk of publishing information they might wish to take back.

Businesses that do not update their computer systems, software, firewalls, or antivirus programs put themselves at great risk of having their system compromised.

Still, there are those who like to see successful people fall.

According to workplacebullying.org, people are targeted because of the perception of a threat. For some reason the bully feels threatened by the target if they:

- Have it together. They're confident, capable, and likeable.

- Have the most skill, at the top of their game.

- Are the elder statesman/woman, the person with the most experience.

- Are more technically skilled.

- Have a desire for nurturing, teaching, and helping others.

Of course, not all targets have these character traits, but there is one thing that is true, the bully will operate with impunity in order to enslave them to their wrath.

In a 2007 Workplace Bullying Institute survey[2], it was discovered that 45 percent of workers who were bullied suffered stress-related health problems.

When the economy tanked in 2008, a lot of people took a big hit. You don't have to look far down a street in Anytown, USA or the world to see its result. People lost money in the stock market, lost jobs; businesses lost clients; and whole industries took a bath. Financial hardship reached into places it never had before. At the same time, a new economy — a digital economy — began to reshape communications, but most had no idea how to figure it out.

Needless to say, a lot of people ended up owing a lot of money and the debt lasted for years. Some were never able to recover.

A person might see a glimmer of hope in their situation, and truly believe they would be able to make amends — pay back everything they owed. They didn't file for bankruptcy because that also required money they didn't have, so the collection calls continued and then the judgments appeared.

Some creditors were sensitive to the fact that they, too, were on shaky ground, so their persistence, even through a collection agency, was not as hard-nosed as others. But then you'd get the odd one who decided to make it so miserable for the debtor that their actions insured the debtor would never be able to repay their debt or anyone else's. The creditor would physically and mentally harass the debtor, then take it to the point where they would broadcast untruths to the Internet for the sole purpose of revenge.

---

2 "Results of the 2007 WBI U.S. Workplace Bullying Survey," WorkplaceBullyingInstitute.org, accessed November, 2014. www.workplacebullying.org/wbiresearch/wbi-2007

In one situation, a creditor's collection agency used a payment attempt against the debtor by using the information on the check to freeze the debtor's bank account for three months after garnisheeing every last penny out of it, thus rendering that business dormant and unable to deposit funds and pay its rent or contractors.

The following numbers show the depth of the credit crisis. It impacts just under 50 percent of the American population in some states. All-consuming debt, coupled with the inability to pay puts many of these people at high risk of cyberbullying, but also at high risk of suicide if the cyberbullying becomes too much to bear.

Over one in three Americans are deep in debt to the point of collections and judgments. This is according to the Urban Institute, which adds that of the approximate 77 million people that owe non-mortgage bills, the average debt-load is $5,178[3].

That may not sound like a lot of money to you, but for someone who hasn't had work for over two years, or has only been able to land a handful of part-time hours since 2008 — it might as well be $500,000. These people earn less than $6,000 a year and many times have families to support[4].

While debt is a problem for the entire country, geographically, the southern states have taken the biggest hit. When you look at the percentage of state residents with debt in collections, the numbers are staggering[5]. The highest is Nevada at 47 percent, with metro Las Vegas at 49 percent.

People in long-term poverty and debt are extremely fragile. Couple the stress with cyberbullying and it might push someone over the edge.

The Great Depression has nothing on today's economy when it comes to suicides[6]. The Centers for Disease Control and Prevention claim that suicide rates rise and fall with the strength of the economy. There are statistics shown in the American Journal of Public Health to bolster this fact.

What is alarming is that since the economic collapse of 2008, there is a higher death rate by suicide than from car crashes. Of course, these numbers are somewhat skewed when factoring in veterans returning

---

3 "Delinquent Debt in America," Urban Institute, accessed November, 2014.
www.urban.org/publications/413191.html
4 "Understanding Poverty," Urban Institute, accessed November, 2014. www.urban.org/poverty/index.cfm
5 "1 in 3 U.S. adults have 'debt in collections'," CNN Money, accessed November, 2014.
http://money.cnn.com/2014/07/29/pf/debt-collections/index.html?iid=HP_LN&hpt=hp_t2
6 "More Americans Committing Suicide than During the Great Depression," WashingtonsBlog.com, accessed November, 2014. www.washingtonsblog.com/2013/05/more-americans-committing-suicide-than-during-the-great-depression.html

from war in the Middle East because most instances are under-reported. The bottom line is, the risk of death is higher by suicide than it is in combat. I think I need to repeat that so it will sink in: The risk of death is higher by suicide than it is in combat.

Unemployment, financial distress, and foreclosure are the triggers for the increase in suicide rates. Statistics show that the people struggling for work are twice as likely to commit suicide over those who are already working. Unemployment leads to depression and a host of negative impacts. Factor in a cyberbully and the risk increases.

1. How High-Profile Individuals become Targets

"You should go die." "You should burn in hell." "You're an idiot." "You cost me money." All things said to someone online[7].

Sadly, it is not uncommon for athletes, actors, musicians, and other high profile people especially to receive such venomous words. They can be continuous, non-stop assaults that literally terrorize one's social media accounts. Not everyone is equipped with a strong sense of self to shrug them off.

This was certainly the case with Canadian tennis player Rebecca Marino. She was already battling depression when the anonymous Internet trolls infiltrated her Twitter and Facebook feeds.

While Marino knew the importance of social media as part of society, the 22-year-old made a decision to leave tennis. Cyberbullying wasn't the only reason, but it probably helped her lose her passion for the game, compounded with her depression[8].

National Hockey League forward Joffrey Lupul also faced the wrath of Twitter, along with his player colleagues. He would try to stay strong while scrolling his feed, but there would be times he'd turn off the account.

British speed skater Elise Christie and Italian skater Arianna Fontana collided on the inside of the short track while in pursuit of a gold medal at the Sochi Olympics. Korea's Park Seung-hi was removed from competition when she became collateral damage to the crash. But when Christie logged into to her Twitter account, she had a steady

---

7 "Rebecca Marino is not alone as a cyberbullied athlete," TheStar.com, accessed November, 2014. www.thestar.com/sports/2013/02/21/rebecca_marino_is_not_alone_as_a_cyberbullied_athlete.html
8 "Rebecca Marino quits tennis following cyberbullying incidents," TheStar.com, accessed November, 2014. www.thestar.com/sports/tennis/2013/02/20/rebecca_marino_quits_tennis_following_cyberbullying_incidents.html

stream of death threats amongst her tweets, mostly from Korean fans. She closed her Twitter account[9].

The end of an event is a vulnerable moment for any athlete. It takes years of sacrifice and training to qualify for an Olympic Games and in Christie's case, the dream ended in a flash, along with those of two other athletes. In that moment when competition ends, losing is hard enough for an athlete. It's not like they can't take criticism, but when venom rolls through their energy, it can forever alter a person.

Everything a high-profile person does is under the microscope. When they step out of their room or house, there are cell phone cameras pointed at them from all angles at every step, just waiting to catch that moment when they falter or pick their nose. When they do, cyberspace erupts and swallows them whole, berating them for being such morons. The vitriol that ensues is enough to pierce through the toughest of shells.

Canadian speed skater Brittany Schussler innocently Tweeted a selfie photo of herself with President Vladimir Putin at the Sochi Olympics — in Russia — where he had invested billions of dollars into the Games. Let's face it, if the president of Russia snuggled up to you for a selfie, you'd probably post it, too. Her Twittersphere exploded.

Three-time Olympic Gold Medalist with the Canadian Women's National Team and television broadcaster Jennifer Botterill said it best in a *Huffington Post* article. "It used to be you'd get yelled at in the arena, but then you could go home. Now it follows you home."

If only all of cyberspace would follow the rules set out by Hockey New Brunswick: "Give yourself 24 hours to cool down before posting a comment."

People can be downright awful. Gary Barlow from the *Take That* show lost his daughter, who was stillborn[10].

He and his wife were mocked about her when they were sent song lyrics on Twitter. In a strange twist of fate, the Internet troll was thought to be Kenneth Tong, a former *Big Brother* contestant.

Olympian Tom Daley's father had died in 2011 from brain cancer. A 17-year-old was issued a harassment warning from Twitter after he sent Daley a Tweet saying that he had let his dad down.

---

9   "Cyberbullying Is Not an Olympic Sport," HuffingtonPost.ca, accessed November, 2014.
    www.huffingtonpost.ca/craig-and-marc-kielburger/cyberbullying_b_4899285.html?just_reloaded=1
10 "Five celebrities who have been victims of web trolls," Itv.com, accessed November, 2014.
    www.itv.com/news/2013-02-22/five-celebrities-who-have-been-victims-of-web-trolls

BBC Sports' Gary Lineker's son George received a Tweet, taunting him about his childhood leukemia. The troll was 21-year-old Mark Sinnott who opined, "pity ya [sic] didn't die," adding that his dad Gary was "washed up" and calling George "leukemia boy."

One morning, entertainment fans opened up their Twitter and Facebook accounts and were shocked to hear the news that one of Glee's leading actors, Chris Colfer, had been fired from the show[11].

The announcement was very convincing: "Due to personal issues, I have been let go from the cast of GLEE. Explanations will come shortly … " but not true.

It was open season on *Glee* actors, when Lea Michele discovered her Twitter account was hacked, too. This tweet announced she was pregnant[12].

Entertainment website JustJared.com created a short piece on Jodie Foster. Accompanying the write-up were pictures of her carrying groceries and another of her feeding a parking meter. The report was about her wanting to direct the show *Orange Is the New Black*.

While the entry was only four small paragraphs and pronounced nothing that could be construed as controversial, the comments were mostly mean, although a couple of people jumped to her defense.

"There is something that people in franc [sic] dislike about Jodie foster … She should stop being such a wannabe." "@___ wasn't she retiring? What a liar she is, what an attention whooore!" "I think most people are not interested in this Woman and her filthy disgusting lifestyle."

Even celebrities — maybe especially celebrities — are not safe from cyberbullies.

---

11 "Chris Colfer Not Fired From Fox's 'Glee,' Says Show Rep (Updated)," TheWrap.com, accessed November, 2014. www.thewrap.com/chris-colfer-fired-from-foxs-glee/?utm_source=newsletter&utm_medium=email&utm_campaign=contactology
12 "'Glee' Hack Attack Hits Lea Michele Over Pregnancy," TheWrap.com, accessed November, 2014. www.thewrap.com/glee-hack-attack-hits-lea-michele-over-pregnancy/?utm_source=newsletter&utm_medium=email&utm_campaign=contactology

4

Can You Stop Cyberbullying before It Happens?

Internet security educator Robert Cairns[1] notes there is one simple place to start when it comes to protecting yourself from cyberbullying: Use common sense.

"Don't take anything you read on the Internet verbatim. Do a quick check to see if stuff [corroborates] ... Educate yourself."

Cairns will watch people's feeds. For example, he suggests if you really want to know the true character of people, look at their Twitter account, even their Facebook feed.

Yngve Hauge asserts that if someone isn't bringing anything positive to your social space, you have the choice to keep him or her out of your connections. Social space is like your house. You ask the negative person to leave. If he or she doesn't leave willingly, you have the person forcibly removed. You have the right to delete a comment or a connection. Just because it is a public forum doesn't give anyone the right to invade it.

---

1   RobertBCairns.com, accessed November, 2014. www.robertbcairns.com

For example, during the course of writing this chapter, a quick glance at my Facebook feed and I noticed a fellow from abroad had posted a video, which played automatically without my having to click on it (which is one of the site's settings). I wasn't sure if it was play acting or real. It was a video of a double hanging from a box where the victims' feet were only about a half a foot from the ground. It seemed very real. I wanted to confirm its intent and copied and pasted the language into Google Translate. The person had only said the act was regrettable.

To carry this further to see if this fellow was a hate-monger, I copied and pasted another bit of text from his feed and through the poor translation, I sensed that the words were negative toward the west. Ambiguous, sure, but the video was enough of a red flag that I reported the post to Facebook and unfriended him, which pulls him and any of his posts out of my feed.

Sometimes, I will put people on caution watch, depending on their posts, which I will hide from my feed. But in this case, this was not the type of person I wanted in my space if his posts were videos of hangings.

When someone adds hateful comments to your posts, including those that egg on others to engage in a verbal altercation or if they are perpetually negative, and he or she does it often enough, unfriend and block the person. We can control our feeds.

If one of your connections is a bully or something just doesn't feel right about the person, don't call him or her out on it. Engaging a bully fuels the fire. Bullies don't react rationally. Bullying the bully or getting your friends to bully the bully only makes you look like the aggressor.

If you notice someone else getting bullied, say something (not to the bully). Give support to the person being bullied.

It is easy for iPredators to rant, judge, and make vicious statements about your business outside of your feed. There doesn't have to be a reason.

1. Monitor and Manage Your Online Presence

Be proactive and monitor your online presence. Google yourself regularly. Search your name and your business's name in the social networks. Even if you don't have a website, any social media presence, and don't even like to use email, you are still at risk for cyberbullying. Someone can still target you online, only it will be the only thing that shows up in your name with nothing to counter it.

The first thing to do is to establish an online presence. And yes, the more one works on the Internet, the more prone they are to nasties that float around in spam, virus attacks, and negative feedback. However, if you Google a business to see if it is legit and nothing shows up, what is the first thought that comes to your mind? What makes you think others are not doing the same to you?

Maximize your online presence.

2. Online Security

Play smart. Don't click a link in that PayPal email or the one that promises you a good deal on web design from the company in India or China. Most of those types of emails are as legitimate as the Nigerian money transfers and the penis enlargement ads. There is probably a more than a 90 percent chance that those links are phishing links, designed to infiltrate your device and capture passwords to your social media, e-commerce, and banking sites.

Identity fraud is a huge issue. There are enough people trying to infiltrate your social media to take over your accounts, you don't need to make it easy — especially if one of those phishers is your bully. It would save him or her the trouble of creating a new hate page for you if he or she can just use your existing page.

Don't click any of those links sent to you for Facebook, Twitter, PayPal, or your bank that say your account has been compromised, or do you know Sarah from high school?

You'll also see direct messages inside Twitter, Facebook, and other sources from people you legitimately know. However, if you are asked to click a link or support a program and it sounds a bit disingenuous, it's more than likely the person's real account has been hacked — the same way yours will be when you click that link. The way to get back control of your social media account is to change your password. Do it now, regardless. Do it often. Schedule yourself to change all of your passwords at least every six months. Yes, it is a pain and yes, I do know how many you have and it probably isn't as many passwords as I have. But change the ones you use most often — the ones at higher risk — on a regular basis.

If yours is a consumer-driven business with point of sale transactions, such as a brick-and-mortar retail store or online store, you should probably invest in a Fort Knox system of security. Don't be the next

Target. The retail franchise was hacked and 70 million customers had their personal information compromised while another 40 million had their credit information stolen. While unconfirmed, it is said that the breach came from a third-party vendor.

Watch out for website redirects. If you're like most people, you bookmark the websites you visit the most, like your bank and Facebook. When you click the bookmark, make sure you check the address to make sure it looks kosher. If your bank says clientonline?~chase.com/facbook.com or any other anomaly, close that browser window, open a new one, directly key in the right address and go directly to your site. Then maybe delete that bookmark and ask your bank how to report phishing issues. Site redirects are another way hackers, phishers, and other scammers lure you to serve up your passwords on a platter.

Surveys are a pain at the best of times but sometimes they are also used to get personal information from you so the recipient can go to town with creating a new identity in your name.

If you plan to purchase merchandise online, including concert tickets, make sure you are logged into a legitimate site. Ticketmaster's cousin Ticketmistress is probably not where you should be inputting your credit card for Clint Black or Macklemore tickets.

Clear your cache daily. Every website you visit leaves a residue in the form of cache images, icons, and other space wasters. Eventually it can impact the performance of your device if you don't clean out the trash regularly. The other thing that can happen is the residue leaves you vulnerable to those lying in wait to find a crack in the foundation.

Make sure your antivirus protection is current and always on in the background, checking the websites you visit, your emails, and anything else you do. Mine even checks my Facebook feed.

Check your smartphone, Facebook, Twitter, and other social media settings and turn off geotagging. Don't share where you are at all times. Don't use location services.

If you forget to turn off geotagging in your cell phone, any picture you take and post will have its location. Don't give crime a chance.

I used to use Foursquare, which is a location-service social media site. I wouldn't check in until after I left a venue, but if you checked in at home, the GPS would lead people right to your doorstep. It's a little unnerving, when you think about it. Yesterday, you checked in at your home-based business. Today you're at the beach on vacation. Hello! Come on in, Mr. Crook!

3. Be Mindful of All That Is Said and Presented in Your Name

Have editorial guidelines for your social media posts, website, and blog and ask your staff to adhere to them. You want to give your community managers some liberty to engage and post interesting related material to what your company is about, but you can avoid the public relations nightmare that IAC faced from the Tweet Heard Around the World[2].

It was one of those "you can't make this stuff up" moments. Justine Sacco, sadly, was a public relations executive for Barry Diller's company IAC and responsible for some very high profile digital media sites. She was en route to her homeland South Africa and sent off a tweet that went viral and inflamed the digital hemisphere while she was in the air during her 12-hour flight. The tweet was "Going to Africa. Hope I don't get AIDS. Just Kidding. I'm White!" [sic]

Her father actually joined forces with those who campaigned to shame her.

Upon her arrival to Cape Town, Sacco learned about the viral venom and that she had been fired by IAC. Her apology to a South African newspaper said, "My greatest concern was this statement reach South Africa first … " [sic]

Not surprising, a spoof account @LOLJustineSacco appeared with the tagline: PR Disaster. Racist idiot. All-around awful. It included a link to the *Huffington Post* story about her mishap.

Of course her real account was no stranger to inappropriate comments, which have been cringeworthy enough to make one wonder why her employer hadn't taken action against her a lot sooner. They could have implemented an editorial guideline that said: don't post anything racist or that will inflame the digital community.

While some of the vitriol against her was quite nasty, this is one case where the target seemed to have no inner filter when penning Tweets. Perhaps she has learned from her experience. In June 2014, she was hired as the Head of PR for Hot or Not, a game where you check

---

2   "'I am ashamed': PR exec who sparked outrage with racist tweet apologizes after she's fired and her own father calls her an 'idiot'," DailyMail.co.uk, accessed November, 2014. www.dailymail.co.uk/news/article-2527913/Justine-Sacco-tweet-Going-Africa-Hope-I-dont-AIDS-causes-Twitter-outrage.html

out photos of people in your GPS circle and vote on whether they are attractive.

Ann-Margaret Carrozza is a New York-based attorney who came up with something to take the editorial guideline to a whole new level. She inserted clauses in pre- and postnuptial agreements to get couples to agree to not post embarrassing or nude pictures or something that would harm the reputation of the other person on the Internet. She spelled out specific fines per infraction[3]

It's an idea that's taken hold. Therapists were also discussing the need for social agreements. It is certainly a consideration, especially if you've gone into business with your spouse. We have also witnessed various forms of cyberbullying when just two non-related business partners part ways.

Of course, if you have employees, having them sign confidentiality agreements that include social media and public relations guidelines and rules is not a bad idea at all.

3   "The Social Media Pre-Nup: Will This Legal Trend Take Off?" SocialMediaToday.com, accessed November, 2014. http://socialmediatoday.com/kayla-minguez/2492141/social-media-pre-nup-will-legal-trend-take

5

When a Post Crosses the Line

If you have to lie, cheat, steal, obstruct, and bully to get your point across, it must not be a point capable of surviving on its own merits.

— STEVEN WEBER

The United States First Amendment[1] is the document by which freedom of speech is protected in the US. It reads: "Congress shall make no law respecting an establishment of religion, or prohibiting the free exercise thereof, or abridging the freedom of speech, or of the press; or the right of the people to peaceably assemble, and to petition the Government for a redress of grievances."

Freedom of speech includes direct words and symbolic actions. It includes the right to not speak; wear a symbol, like an arm band to protest war; to use offensive words for a political message; and participate in symbolic speech, like burning the flag[2].

---

1 "Bill of Rights," Archives.gov, accessed November, 2014. www.archives.gov/exhibits/charters/bill_of_rights_transcript.html
2 "What Does Free Speech Mean?," United States Courts, accessed December, 2014. www.uscourts.gov/educational-resources/get-involved/constitution-activities/first-amendment/free-speech.aspx

Where the First Amendment cannot be applied is when someone incites action to hurt someone; makes or distributes materials deemed obscene; demonstrate against a war by burning a draft card; is a student who publishes an objection to the school administration in a school newspaper, or says something obscene during a speech, or advocates illegal drug use in a school-sponsored event.

The Canadian Charter of Rights and Freedoms[3] states that "2. Everyone has the following fundamental freedoms: b) freedom of thought, belief, opinion, and expression, including freedom of the press and other media of communication."

The Charter spells out some legal rights: "7. Everyone has the right to life, liberty, and security of the person and the right not to be deprived thereof in accordance with the principals of fundamental justice. ... 12. Everyone has the right not to be subjected to cruel and unusual treatment or punishment."

When you look at the rights afforded every citizen in North America, if the distinction between a salacious post with the intent to injure is clear, then it might be perceived as a violation of the First Amendment or the Charter of Rights and Freedom rather than falling under freedom of speech.

Dr. Michael Nuccitelli has some strong opinions when it comes to using the free speech card to justify acrimony in a legal battle.

"I think free speech is used so loosely nowadays. I don't want the government or anybody up in my butt telling me what I can and I can't say."

That being said, with information technology and the Internet, let's revisit the three ways that you can interact with information:

- Compile it.

- Disseminate it.

- Exchange it.

Nuccitelli summates, "It seems too liberal for someone to say that it is okay for someone to completely defame you, short of talking about child pornography, or being totally obscene with not being taken into consideration the psychological damage it has on others. That is where society has yet to understand the psychological ramifications of adult cyberbullying."

---

3   *Constitution Act, 1982,* Government of Canada Justice Laws Website, accessed December, 2014.
    http://laws-lois.justice.gc.ca/eng/const/page-15.html

A lot of times people will tell you, don't worry about it. It's not a big deal. Turn it off. That constant minimization adds to the target's feelings of isolation.

The thing about cyberspace is that we all use it, and some of us use it as much as we breathe. Nobody is perfect, either. Whether it's online or offline, we've all done things we wish we could take back. When we finally learn the truth, that what we said or did was uncalled for and hurtful, sometimes we are embarrassed to admit our wrongs, take it back, and make amends. I know I have done things I'm not proud of. I've hurt some people with my words online, and for that I'm truly sorry. I'm sure karma has paid me back a couple of times for my actions.

If we have posted something we'd like to take back, we can find it and delete it. It may still appear in the Internet archives, but hopefully it will get buried as time moves on.

Maybe at the time of our actions they could be construed as bullying. But now that we know better, we do better. A cyberbully with the character traits Dr. Nuccitelli has described is not contrite, nor do they care if they ruin their target. They might even enjoy it if their target internalizes their actions to the point of contemplating or attempting suicide. Who knows?

Actor Jonah Hill felt enormous guilt after hurling a gay slur at a tabloid photographer[4] who threw insults at him and his family. Hill's response was it was all he could think of saying in the moment that would be hurtful. He realized his intent was to hurt more than anything, but he apologized because "words have weight and meaning." Besides on *The Tonight Show with Jimmy Fallon*, Hill also apologized for his actions on *The Howard Stern Show*.

1. Trolls

The most well-meaning post will attract haters. The Internet community calls these people trolls. You see them assault a feed with hate-mongering and garbage. For example, in looking at a YouTube video, like the band everyone seems to love to hate: Nickelback's "Savin' Me" from the official Nickelback VEVO channel[5].

You don't have to scroll down far in the comments to find this:

---

4   "Jonah Hill Gives Emotional Apology on Jimmy Fallon (VIDEO)," Variety.com, accessed December, 2014.
    http://variety.com/2014/tv/news/jonah-hill-gives-emotional-apology-on-jimmy-fallon-video-1201211851
5   "Nickelback - Savin' Me" YouTube.com, accessed December, 2014. http://youtu.be/SvBu3AQpBTw

"You should understand that this is the butthole of youtube. [sic] This song is terrible. You clearly are not in touch with real human emotion if you believe this to be in any way deep or meaningful, May god have mercy on your soul you stupid … "

I admit that when I looked at a few other videos of popular artists (John Legend and Zakk Wylde of Black Label Society), the comments had been cleaned up and sanitized.

There was much flak about Google (which owns YouTube) forcing users to create a Google+ account in an effort to keep them from hiding behind anonymity. It didn't really stop the trolls because many of them just created fake Google accounts. However, just before I finished this book, I had to go to YouTube to delete a comment that was posted to one of my videos: "wtf dont make videos old woman."

Twitter is one of the worst places for trolls because it is more difficult to manage. Even #puppies aren't safe in this one tweet I saw: "I had a dream I had two puppies and then this man eating hippo ate them maybe that's a sign."

Most Wordpress websites and blogs allow you to customize or control which comments show up from the back end. For those who are still building an audience, sometimes you might be reluctant to turn off comments or have them go into a queue for approval for fear of missing a legitimate one. This is a warranted concern, especially if you look at your own behavior.

There are some of us who may want to comment on a post, but if we are not already a logged-in member of the site, we won't bother to comment if we have to set up yet another profile and password. By opening the feed up for everyone, a site will get inundated with spam. There might be a happy medium where you can approve proven commenters and the rest fall into a cue for moderation.

This is now the case for the popular media site Gawker.com, which is the parent company of another popular site: Jezebel.com. Jezebel had to publicly call out Gawker[6] for allowing trolls to bomb its comment feed with rape GIFs. Jezebel employees were distraught that Gawker's moderator allowed fake "burner" accounts to infiltrate the website by posting horrible images with the Jezebel logo overlaid.

Here is an example of just how cruel and heartless people can be when hiding behind an anonymous account. Zelda Williams, the

6 "Gawker Media Changes Policies in Wake of Jezebel's Scathing Open Letter," TheWrap.com, accessed December, 2014. www.thewrap.com/gawker-media-changes-policies-in-wake-of-jezebels-scathing-open-letter

daughter of the late comedian Robin Williams, was faced with abuse in social media immediately after her father's death[7].

It is hard to imagine the depth of inhumanity and depravity someone might harbor to bully someone who is raw in pain. You have to wonder if they would say and share the same things to their face. To her credit, Zelda Williams didn't delete or deactivate her account. She chose to take a break from it in order to shield herself from the rancor.

When Anthony Elonis publicly threatened to kidnap and kill his wife on Facebook in 2010, the United States Supreme Court would not accept his claim[8] for free speech. He was slapped with a 44-month sentence.

Elonis claimed his posts were his own lyrics written to mimic others that were penned by famed rapper Eminem. The case argued the difference between a perceived online threat versus art. As of this writing, Elonis' case is in front of the Supreme Court, who will determine if violent posts should be considered real threats[9].

Separating intended violence from art is one of those sticky areas where the First Amendment and the Charter of Rights and Freedoms could go either way.

Talking trash about someone may or may not be considered cyberbullying, and it may be the same with threats and harassment. Whenever something happens that taps into our emotions — the more controversial and polarizing it is — the more you can expect an inappropriate comment.

Travis Crabtree lists a few examples of posts gone bad[10], where the law was forced to step in.

- A New York Knicks fan posts naked pictures of himself with a gun while suggesting the team's owner has to die.

- Using someone else's name without permission to create a web page or message on a social media site.

- Creating a web page, social media page, or post with the intention to harm, defraud, intimidate, and threaten someone.

---

7 "Zelda Williams Leaves Social Media After Receiving Abuse Over Her Father's Death," Buzzfeed.com, accessed December, 2014. www.buzzfeed.com/catesevilla/zelda-williams-leaves-social-media-after-receiving- abuse-fol
8 "When Does Music Become a Criminal Threat?," ThinkProgress.org, accessed December, 2014. http://thinkprogress.org/justice/2014/06/19/3450412/how-real-are-threats-made-on-social-media
9 "Supreme Court Facebook Case 2014: Anthony Elonis Lawsuit Asks Whether Violent Posts Should Be Considered Real Threats," International Business Times, accessed December, 2014. www.ibtimes.com/supreme-court-facebook-case-2014-anthony-elonis-lawsuit-asks-whether-violent-posts-1731213
10 "When Online Behavior Crosses the Line The Law on Threats, Libel and Just Being Rude," eMediaLaw.com, accessed December, 2014. www.emedialaw.com/when-online-behavior-crosses-the-line-the-law-on-threats-libel-and-just-being-rude

- Sending electronic communication using someone's contact details and personal information under false pretenses.

- Publishing private nude photographs or video (revenge porn) with a person's contact details and personal information.

If someone with a reasonable mind could believe the author of a post intends to do harm, that takes a post from free speech to an actual threat.

2. Good versus Evil

There are times the Internet is used for good and moments it is used for hate. Many occasions those intentions collide to the point where one side reigns over the other.

@OpieRadio shock jock Anthony Cumia from the Opie and Anthony show accused a woman of assaulting him in Times Square and proceeded to post her photo and pen a diatribe[11] of racially incendiary tweets. Cumia was taking pictures and claimed the African-American didn't want her picture taken, so she accosted him.

After the Cumia story hit the Twittersphere, he was duly fired by SiriusXM, while many of his fans responded by cancelling their accounts in support, which included posting pictures of their cancellation notices.

When a video of the brutal execution of American photojournalist James Foley was circulated on the Internet[12] by the militant group ISIS, there was a backlash of digital citizens who used their voice to blacklist further circulation with the hashtags #RespectJamesFoley, #ISISmediaBlackout and #condemnIsis. Tom Doran (@portraitinflesh) said it best in his tweet:

"Don't share the video. Don't share the pictures. Don't work for ISIS. Share images of James Foley's life instead. #ISIS"

Twitter also took action and removed all tweets that had embedded the video or screenshots. Twitter CEO Dick Costolo messaged, "We have been and are actively suspending accounts as we discover them related to this graphic imagery."

---

11 "Angry Anthony Cumia Fans Cancel SiriusXM Subscriptions After Firing Over Racist Tweets," TheWrap.com, accessed December, 2014. www.thewrap.com/angry-anthony-cumia-fans-cancel-siriusxm-subscriptions-after-firing-over-racist-tweets/?utm_source=newsletter&utm_medium=email&utm_campaign=contactology
12 "James Foley: How social media is fighting back against Isis propaganda," TheGuardian.com, accessed December, 2014. www.theguardian.com/technology/2014/aug/20/james-foley-how-social-media-is-fighting-back-against-isis-propaganda

If bullies, trolls, and their believers would consider context before they respond to something, the nastiness on the Internet might get cut in half.

Breanna Mitchell was not unlike any of us when we visit a place of profound historical importance. So when she took a picture of herself with Auschwitz behind her[13] and posted it on the Internet, people freaked out and countered her #AuschwitzSelfie with doctored images of her against historically terrible images.

What people didn't bother to learn was that she was a student of World War II and Holocaust history. She took the picture to honor her father, who spawned her interest in the topic.

The thing is, we all take pictures everywhere we go, and share them. We all take selfies against a backdrop to prove we were there, if anything else, for our own archives. It's what makes us social beings. It's what makes us human.

3. Church Closes Food Bank Because It Attracts Poor People

This salacious headline has riled up a lot of Facebook goers. It is a typical scenario, though. Before getting vetted, the story spreads virally, then someone actually Googles it and by sifting through the source of the links to find one that is more credible, it can't be found. For this link, unless the Ottawa Citizen or some other source took down the link, it is difficult to prove. I discovered this story in an August 2014 Facebook feed, which showed a photograph of the newspaper story. It looked credible, but there was no date on it.

If this article is true, there is no libel, but there is a lot of questioning of faith. If this story is untrue, this is a highly libelous statement, besmirching the church and its minister. However, it is difficult to find the original source, considering the links go back as far as 2011.

4. A Word About Poor Marketing That Crosses the Line

Lately there seem to be a lot of overzealous headlines from reputable websites claiming something outrageous, but when you click on the

---

13 "'Auschwitz Selfie' Outrage: But You're Supposed to Take Pictures," TheWrap.com, accessed December, 2014. www.thewrap.com/auschwitz-selfie-outrage-but-youre-supposed-to-take-pictures/?utm_source=newsletter&utm_medium=email&utm_campaign=contactology

link to open the article, there is nothing in the piece that confirms the story. In fact, the very opposite is true. Official sources will be quoted in the story, denying what the headline had written as fact.

Here is an example from a well-known sports television website: "NHL expansion a 'done deal'." When you open the article, the NHL commissioner blatantly denies the expansion is a done deal. This is headline writing to get you to click or viral a post before you read it. It could be classified as Troll Advertising.

Here is a version of troll email advertising in Sample 1.

Sample 1
Troll Advertising

5. When You Decide the Line Has Been Crossed

When something comes into your email or social media inbox that makes you feel uncomfortable or looks like a creep (such as Facebook spammers who profess their love for you), this could be more than just spam or a phisher seeking to infiltrate your account. It could be a scam baiter. This is a huge business where someone from an overseas country tries to get you to chat with them, to lure you into an online "relationship" where eventually he or she will make up a story to get you to send money. Delete these and report them as spam.

When someone messages you with a threat, whether it is in a direct message or in a comment feed, see the next chapter.

If someone says something highly inappropriate to you or in general in your public comment feed, delete the comment. Depending on the post, the pattern of behavior (which you can check on his or her feed), or whether the person is just "off" today, you can decide whether it warrants blocking them from your account. Sometimes it is a friend who provides you value most of the time, but sometimes they get carried away. It may not be a blocking sin.

When you see something written about you that is not true or something has been embellished to intentionally hurt you or your business, proceed to the next chapter.

6

When You Discover You Are the Target of a Cyberbully

1. You've Been Cyber Attacked: Now What?

Here's the scenario. You Google yourself and notice that someone, maybe even someone you know, has said something awful and nasty about you and it shows up in the first page because the perpetrator has done a good job of using keywords that relate to the places you go on the Web.

There will likely be a physical response that immediately happens which you have no control over: You will feel the adrenaline pumping fluids from your body to the top of your head. Your ears might start ringing. You could even hyperventilate. You might go into a bit of shock, stunned, trying to soak it all in.

It's bad. It's really bad. It's also the only time you've ever experienced such an attack. There have been disagreements but never something intentionally geared to bring you down.

1.1 Stay calm

The first rule of thumb is to keep calm. Do not respond. Keep your emotions in check.

Go through all your links in Google to see if there is anything more. Then Google yourself with the subject's name. Does anything more show up? Go to your main social media links and do the same. Search your name with the perpetrator's.

When you are sure you've found it all, the next step is to record the evidence.

1.2 Document

Your first instinct is to make it disappear, but you need to document the heck out of everything. Do not delete anything.

Regardless of what device you are working from, there is one beautiful certainty each has: the ability to take screenshots. If you're not sure how to take a screenshot from your device, Google "how do I take screenshots with Samsung Chromebook" or whatever you are using.

Save the screenshots to your device and back them up. Include any conversations in the feed, such as on a Facebook post. In that conversation, there may be others looking to branch out the assault.

If your cyberbully is emailing you, report the person to your Internet service provider. Forward the entire email or series of them to your ISP.

You can also save conversations in Skype chat, Google chat, and others, which can either be copied and pasted into a text or Word document or downloaded as a text file. I would also take a screenshot of what it looks like in Skype.

For more detailed information about how to properly document your case, see Chapter 10.

1.3 Tell somebody

This one is tricky. Tell somebody you trust, who is on your side, not someone who will judge you based on what this person posted. Get a second opinion to see if the person is interpreting the posts, emails, and situation the same way you are.

If you counter the claim publicly, you are putting attention on the post, and there will be those who believe the bad, even if you considered them friends.

1.4 Find out who owns the website where the post was made

Find out who owns or hosts the website where the post was made. Maybe you can ask them to delete it. Don't hold your breath, but you can try.

If the website is a public site, like a social media website, report the post and flag it for investigation, asking to have it removed. This may not work either, but it's worth a try.

Tell the web administrator you are filing a police report.

It is not easy to get disparaging content taken down from a website. Some website owners refuse without a court order. Sometimes you can prove your case without having to go the legal route. As you learned in the case of Jennifer Miller-Bender, getting a page removed from Facebook can take time.

If your bully is a former mate, you can only hope there are no pictures of you, real or doctored, in compromising positions. Such was not the case with a Houston woman. Her ex-friend created a fake page and posted doctored pornographic material to insert the face of his target. The woman was made aware when her friends and family were invited to join.

This woman decided to sue Facebook for $123 million[1] when it took the social media giant several months to remove the revenge pornographic page.

1.5 Block the cyberbully

Block everyone associated with the post, including those who jumped on the bandwagon in the comment feed. Block them on all your social sites, email, and anywhere you can find them on a mutual platform. Make sure you have done all your screenshots first because once you block them, you won't be able to see their posts anymore.

---

1 "Facebook Slapped With $123 Million Lawsuit Over 'Revenge Porn' Page," TheWrap.com, accessed November, 2014. www.thewrap.com/facebook-slapped-with-123-million-lawsuit-over-revenge-porn-page/?utm_source=newsletter&utm_medium=email&utm_campaign=contactologytnotes

1.6 Legal advice

Find a legal service that can relate to cyberbullying issues in your jurisdiction. There is a strong chance there won't be anyone. It's such a new area, that depending on where you live, the local lawyers may not even know who to refer you to. Search online for legal advice with respect to this issue in your area. Find out what laws have been broken.

If posts are made on international websites, expect a tougher time as international cross-border laws have not caught up with the Internet age.

If the issue is ongoing harassment, see about applying for an order of protection. Before you take the steps to sue, perhaps your lawyer could draft up a cease and desist letter, ordering the bully to take down his or her posts.

To sue or not to sue: There is no guarantee you will win, no matter how blatant the defamation might be. If you still decide to move forward with a lawsuit, expect the process to be long and drawn out, expensive, and there will be damaging testimony if you have not been living your life as a saint. The bully could be Charles Manson and you will still be the one with your life on display.

The world could look at you as the attacker when you sue. Regardless of who ultimately wins the case, the damage will have compounded as the testimony is circulated online. Suing will not restore your reputation.

But if you do pursue legal action, there may also be a statute of limitations. In Canada, you have two years. In the United States, it can be one to three years, depending on which state you're in[2].

How bad is the assault? Does the damage warrant the fight? What laws have been broken? You'll need to determine who to sue. It isn't always cut and dried. If something has been shared and re-shared, find the original source of the defamation. If the posts were anonymous, you're going to have to find out who the people are. Are they in your jurisdiction? If not, you will have to consider if suing internationally is worth the bother, especially if the source is from a country like Russia or Bahrain where there may or may not be cooperation for another country's legal team. You will probably need to sue in the location of where the iPredator lives. So even in the US or Canada, if you live in California or Saskatchewan and the perpetrator lives in Texas or Ontario, you will have to find a legal team that is licensed to practice in those

---

2 "Time Limits to File a Defamation Lawsuit," AllLaw.com, accessed November, 2014.
   www.alllaw.com/articles/nolo/personal-injury/defamation-lawsuit-statutes-limitation-state-chart.html

jurisdictions. You will have to travel to the other location when it comes time for trial. It will be an extremely expensive proposition without any assurance that you will win.

1.7 Report it to the police

As with the lawyer, your local police station may not have heard of such a thing. Report it anyway. Get a case file number, in case you decide to sue for defamation. Unless your life is in imminent danger, it may be unlikely that the police will get involved. If your business is being affected, you might be able to get the police to issue a warning, but that is something they may tell you to do through a lawyer.

2. What Not to Do

The first thing you must do is DO NOT email, call, or respond in any way directly or indirectly to the bully. Do not get any of your friends to respond.

There are a few reasons why this is important:

1. Bullies live for your response. Nothing you can ever say or do may make the person apologize or remove the post. What it will do is egg him or her on to do more damage. The more you argue, the more you look like the bully. Believe me, the bully will milk that for all it's worth. He or she does not care about what the fallout will be to you. That is why the bully did it in the first place.

2. When you ignore the bully, it shows them that you do not consider them of any importance.

3. Move on. Make sure you set up a Google Alert for your name and perhaps your name with the cyberbully's name, but then, once you go through the process of documentation and preparing yourself for a legal fight, move on with your life. Later on we'll discuss how to do that. For now, the best thing you can do for yourself is carry on business as usual. Even if your business lives online and your digital footprint is essential to finding new business, carry on as if nothing ever happened. Only respond when someone else brings it up, but have your talking points ready. Do not bully the bully, so be careful of the words you choose. Don't even let his or her name pass through your lips. Erase the bully as if he or she were a squashed bug on the windshield of your car and you're holding the power spray.

7

The Short-Term and Long-Term Effects of Being Cyberbullied

1. Top Model Charlotte Dawson

Charlotte Dawson was a popular judge on the television show *Australia's Next Top Model* and a model from Auckland, New Zealand. She was considered one of the most beautiful women across the globe and was celebrated in her own country. (www.itv.com/news/2013-02-22/five-celebrities-who-have-been-victims-of-web-trolls/)

Like many entrepreneurs are the face of their company, Dawson's face was her brand. She was known for her especially blunt critique of aspiring up and coming models that appeared on the show.

In 2012, Twitter trolls bullied her and prodded her to kill herself, and they convinced her to try.

After her recovery, Dawson campaigned to address the issue of cyberbullying and its risks. But that message backfired. Because of her persona on her television show, she was bullied even more. Still, Dawson continued to run her anti-bullying campaign. Yet despite its success, the popularity of her show, and that she was living the dream, on February 22, 2014, she finally succeeded in suicide. The trolls had won.

2. Recognizing the Emotions You'll Experience

"You hurt someone and leave a scar," Yngve Hauge remarks. "The people who are bullied sometimes can't rebuild those scars."

Hauge admits he kept to himself for several years. He hid behind a mask. But he does recognize that if he had come out earlier about his being the victim of a bully, he might not have had some of the problems he encountered. He recommends that you at least tell one person your story.

Dianne Ojar-Ali describes the feeling as a quiet and private thing, even though you've been besmirched across the Internet.

"You take it emotionally as opposed to logically. You get angry and frustrated. There is hurt. There is confusion. The first thing is emotion kicks in. You lose sense of what you need to do."

It is as if you have to constantly watch your back. People are jealous. People are hateful, and they use words which can hurt deeply.

Someone could be angry or jealous and want to get back at you. People will especially try to hurt you by making it public. Technology makes it possible to do it in an instant.

Although this is more commonly spoken about on the personal level, it is not easy to find access to organizations for help if you're a business or entrepreneur going through this.

2.1 The emotional stages of defamation

The emotional stages of defamation[1] are:

- First: disbelief, shock, and horror.

- Second: Inquisitiveness.

- Third: Brush-off, as in "will anyone believe it?"

- Fourth: Reality — yes, this can really hurt you.

- Fifth: If the victim stays rational, positive action.

---

1 "The Psychology of Defamation Victims," Dancing with Lawyers, accessed December, 2014. www.dancingwithlawyers.com/defamation/psychology-of-defamation.html

Depending on one's mindset and self-esteem, coupled with the severity of the defamation, the target will:

- Use ability to reason.

- Let anxiety and the denigration torment and imprison him or her.

Even if your emotions run wild with depression, fear, anger, and paranoia, you eventually work through them and mull it out in your mind as to what you can do to combat this. Will doing nothing make it disappear? Will suing the bully get me restitution?

The anxiety of this may weigh so heavily that you may become unbalanced. You either lash out and become a bully yourself, or you withdraw into a dangerous depression.

Lashing out might include emailing or counter-posts of calling out the bully in no uncertain terms, elevating an argument to the point of using violent words and threats. It is also possible the anger could spill out into the physical world by authoring a crime against the bully.

If someone is already emotionally fragile, these are the people who withdraw and are at risk for doing something drastic, like suicide.

There is a learned helplessness that comes with being the target of a cyberbully. Our first reaction is to declare our innocence.

Even as a kid, bullying doesn't go away. It stays with us. People internalize the hate and the pain. As adults, some continue to bully, while others continue to internalize pain. When it happens to adults, they feel vulnerable and exploited.

When it's a business (meaning entrepreneur, business entity, business executive, high profile figure whose face is their brand) that is targeted, there seems to be a stigma that goes along with being defamed. Perhaps that is because marketing is a key component. To have outlandish comments and posts that show up front and center in Google is devastating to a business' credibility, which is the point of the cyberbully. The bully does not care what the repercussions are for you. He or she wants you to suffer. He or she wants people who read it to pile on and continue to perpetuate the abuse. The action is based on spite and malice, period.

Dianne Ojar-Ali observes, "I think everybody is afraid to talk about it. What do you think people's biggest fear is? What other people think of them. Why do you think we keep hiding it? We avoid our negative emotions. We hide it because of what people might think of us. We take it at face value because we don't believe in ourselves. We don't have the confidence to be who we are. I know I didn't do that. I know I'm not like this."

Adults try to hide the fact they've been cyberbullied. Maybe part of the fear is if they point it out to someone, that person will question them as to why someone might be targeting them. A lot of times, you don't know. But perhaps it is a result of something you did, or didn't do. Regardless of what that might be, does that still warrant someone being able to bully you and try to impact your business?

Everything people do is not black and white. There are grey areas around many decisions that are made. Still, owners spend a lifetime building their company and brand, so even if the bullying is against a corporation, it is personal.

There are many health issues that can develop as a result of bullying[2]:

- Severe anxiety that consumes your every waking hour to the point of everywhere you turn, you expect to see some residue fallout or evidence of the cyberbully.

- It could keep you awake at night.

- Your concentration might be shot.

- You could having trouble remembering things.

- People might notice your mood swings.

- You might have moments where you just explode in anger or mope around in a depressed state.

- You could be perpetually sad.

- You might experience heart palpitations.

- You could develop hypertension.

- You might obsess over what has happened to the point that you can't move forward.

- You could have nightmares and flashbacks or the issue keeps jumping into your thoughts when you're trying to do something else.

2 "WBI Survey: Workplace Bullying Health Impact," Workplace Bullying Institute, accessed December, 2014. www.workplacebullying.org/2012/08/09/2012-d

- You might lose your emotional connection.

- You could become severely depressed.

- You might experience terrible headaches; your asthma might be wonky; or you decide to smoke, drink, or drug yourself to mask the pain.

Bullying is really psychological harassment or violence[3]. Here are more psychological conditions that may result from these experiences:

- Debilitating anxiety.

- Panic attacks.

- Clinical depression.

- PTSD (Post-Traumatic Stress Disorder).

- Shame.

- Guilt.

- Overwhelming sense of injustice.

3. The Psychological Price of Being a Businessperson

Nobody knows what goes on behind closed doors. To the outside world, a business could look like a smashing success[4]. There might be rave reviews about the CEO and stories about the millions of dollars raised, launching the business to the top 500 of Forbes' list. But the CEO has a secret. The company is actual teetering on the edge of financial ruin and the CEO is about to have a nervous breakdown from the stress of keeping it together, for appearance's sake.

This is probably the reason why so few of you have heard about business cyberbullying until you opened up this book.

Entrepreneurs do not want to show signs of vulnerability. That is too taboo. It's a cutthroat world and if a CEO shows weakness, competitors circle the Rolodex like sharks, itching to grab any scrap of sales.

What companies might call weakness, social psychiatrists call impression management; the "fake it 'til you make it" syndrome.

---

3   BullyBusters.org, accessed December, 2014. www.bullybusters.org
4   "The Psychological Price of Entrepreneurship," Inc.com, accessed December, 2014.
     www.inc.com/magazine/201309/jessica-bruder/psychological-price-of-entrepreneurship.html

The life of a businessperson is quite vulnerable, fraught with count-less setbacks. There is a juggling of roles, sleepless nights, crippling anxiety, depression, and exhausting fear. Even during the good times, there is a niggle in the back of the neck that reminds them of the days in the abyss.

For many small businesses, any little setback can be devastating financially. An accident can show its impact a year later, after the busi-ness scrambled to find funds to pay everyday bills. Entrepreneurs will max out their lines of credit. They will cash in their 401Ks, Registered Retirement Savings Plans, and whole life insurance values. They'll use their credit cards to pay other credit cards or bills. They'll exhaust ev-ery resource they can think of until they take the next step: humbling themselves, which is like admitting defeat, to borrow money from their parents, kids, other family members, or friends[5].

One of the reasons for the deep-seeded feelings of depression is that business owners feel like their identity is tied to the businesses. So if the business fails, they are a failure.

It is not a stretch for these feelings to transcend to thoughts of suicide.

In both the United States and Canada, there are over 10 suicides for every 100,000 people[6]. The World Health Organization shows that in 2009, the highest percentage of those who died of intentional self-harm were age 35 to 54 (15,277 US/1730 Canada), then age 55 to 74 (8726 US/872 Canada), then 25 to 34 (5720 US/556 Canada).

The University of Oxford and the London School of Hygiene and Tropical Ministry published that people who are on unemployment are 2.5 times more likely to commit suicide[7].

The New Health Guide doesn't cite the source of their findings on Highest Suicide Rate by Profession[8], but they show medical profes-sionals are at the top of the list for white men and women, however sales-related jobs, where the female is exposed to male dominance and sexual harassment puts white women at the second highest rate. For black men and women, the highest rate of suicide is in law enforce-ment, but sales is also a factor for black women.

---

5 "My Darkest Hour," Inc.com, accessed December, 2014. www.inc.com/magazine/201309/jessica-bruder/ inc.500-ceos-share-advice-from-darkest-moments.html?cid=readmore
6 "Here Are The Countries With The Worst Suicide Rates," BusinessInsider.com, accessed December, 2014. www.businessinsider.com/world-suicide-rate-map-2014-4
7 "Global recession linked to 10,000 'economic suicides' across North America and Europe: study," FinancialPost.com, accessed December, 2014. http://business.financialpost.com/2014/06/12/recession-suicide-study
8 "Highest Suicide Rate by Profession," NewHealthGuide.org, accessed December, 2014. www.newhealthguide.org/Highest-Suicide-Rate-By-Profession.html

Collectively, the fallout from cyberbullying is really a form of PTSD. According to the Canadian Mental Health Association (www.cmha.ca), PTSD causes intrusive symptoms, such as re-experiencing the traumatic event. Many people have vivid nightmares, flashbacks, or thoughts of the event that seem to come out of nowhere. They often avoid things that remind them of the event … can make people feel very nervous or 'on edge' all the time. Many feel startled very easily, have a hard time concentrating, feel irritable, or have problems sleeping well. They may often feel something terrible is about to happen.

Most targets suffer in silence. They won't disclose the fact they are being bullied, let alone how they feel about it.

Sara Hawkins is a social media and business lawyer in Phoenix, Arizona. She surmises the reason we don't hear as much about suicides or the fallout to the business community is, "You don't have a community that's been mobilized behind you. You're a single voice. Cyberbullies have a community. There are underworld communities you can go into — chat rooms and such — look what I did, and there are people who will pile on."

She mentioned a situation with a restaurant that was using a pay-per-click advertisement. Competitors were clicking, which would boost the cost of the ad to the restaurant, and then they got off the ad so there wouldn't be any sales. It happens in the Yelp reviews and Google doesn't know if it's the business owner, the competitor, or an employee.

"If I wanted to do a write-up on a restaurant, all I'd have to do is create a fake email, be able to verify it, and say my hours are 'I'm closed on Mondays.' If Mondays were your biggest day, you'd wonder why you weren't getting any customers."

You can see how mean people can be in comments on things and how quickly something innocent can turn into something vile. Entrepreneurs have to put themselves out on a limb and it is so difficult to solicit new business and raise money for projects. It doesn't help when the guy with the fake account is getting tens of thousands of dollars on a crowdfunding site, while the fellow with the legitimate product has to fight hard for a pittance.

"It is commercial terrorism," declares Hawkins. "Large businesses have a team of people to deal with this stuff. Even larger companies are trying to take ownership of the negativity in an attempt to control it."

4. Financial Impact on Business

There are real-world implications of bullying in the workplace[9].

The schoolyard bullies don't change their behavior when they become adults. When you look at the statistics for workplace bullying, the question might be: Who hasn't been bullied in the workplace? As it turns out, not many.

According to a study by VitalSmarts, which polled about 3,000 people, 96 percent said they experienced workplace bullying. Ninety-six percent! Over three-fifths had their work or reputations sabotaged; over 50 percent received threats and intimidation; and four percent were physically assaulted. These statistics do not include sexual harassment.

We know some businesses have anti-harassment policies, but if you've ever reported an infraction, the response is not always in the accuser's favor.

Cyberbullying impacts a target's confidence and his or her digital footprint. It can cost a person a job, infringe on current employment status, and jar the overall aspect of a person's livelihood.

The founder of the Campaign Against Workplace Bullying Gary Namie, PhD, did a study[10] in 1998 out of the University of Northern Carolina at Chapel Hill.

In his findings, he noted that 82 percent of those bullied in the workplace leave their place of employment — 38 percent for health reasons, 44 percent because of a manipulated performance appraisal system. Replacing a person costs two to three times their salary. A survey of 9,000 employees, showed the economic impact of the 57 percent that were harassed was $180 million in lost time and productivity.

There are a number of statistics on workplace bullying and its impact. This doesn't necessarily include cyberbullying, but if we look at the economics of this type of harassment, it would be easy to translate similar numbers towards a company or entrepreneur to whom a digital footprint is equally as important to the business.

In a 2010 and 2007 US Workplace Bullying survey, targeted individuals said the bullying stopped[11] when they left their place of employment.

---

9   "The Real-World Implications Of Workplace And Cyber Bullying," Forbes.com, accessed December, 2014.
    www.forbes.com/sites/meghanbiro/2014/07/27/the-real-world-implications-of-workplace-and-cyberbullying
10 "Workplace bullying web sites, information, resources and links in Canada," BullyOnline.org,
    accessed December, 2014. www.bullyonline.org/workbully/canada.htm
11 "The WBI Website 2011 Instant Poll-B Post-Bullying Financial Woes for Bullied Targets," Workplace Bullying
    Institute, accessed December, 2014. www.workplacebullying.org/multi/pdf/2011-IP-B.pdf

In the aftermath, 26 percent of the targets reported their jobs were never replaced; 25 percent found a safer job for less money; 17 percent found another job for more money but were bullied again; 13.7 percent were bullied again when they got another job for less money; 11.6 percent were able to land a better paying job in a safer environment; and 5.9 percent saw no change in a new job. When you tally that up, it means 53 percent experienced a financial setback and a quarter of them were unable to find replacement work.

5. Can Your Business Recover?

Dianne Ojar-Ali counsels that as a target, you have to rise above the bullying somehow. There is no failure in moving forward.

"There is no failure. There are no mistakes. No regrets. There are only lessons to learn. We can't stop anybody from what they are going to do, but you can turn that around."

Ojar-Ali helped me come to an understanding when it came to business cyberbullying and how it has happened to me. This was something I personally had to go through to find a new direction. It did come with a heavy price, but if I could appreciate what I went through, then I could understand that I was chosen for this. I have a voice and can use my talent, creativity, and resources to help others.

But first, like everyone else, I had to accept it.

"One of the steps is denial: 'What is wrong with me?' Turn it back around. Wish the best. Don't feed the negativity."

Ojar-Ali is right. We don't have to allow someone else to hold us prisoner just because of what he or she wrote about us.

8

How Bullies Roll

Even though the Internet has been around for at least 27 years, it has only been in the last 10 or so that is has it become a part of our day-to-day living. Still, the laws haven't come close to catching up with the technology.

Dr. Michael Nuccitelli summates that the judicial system and law enforcement also don't take into consideration psychological torture.

"They tend to look at everything in a black and white physical standpoint. Now with cyberspace and anonymity, well, they say just turn off the Internet. I'll get a call from a mom, and learning all the hoops they've jumped through (to hold their child's cyberbully accountable). Their loved ones and their support systems will have told them to just turn it off or cancel Facebook."

This attitude does not help the family, especially after they've already gone through the judicial system or filed a report with law enforcement. Now they feel completely isolated.

Unless you've been the target of an attack, it is hard to fathom the sense of vulnerability one feels, even as the head of a corporation. We are supposed to be in control of our own media, but what if the media we control works against us?

Cyberbullying is not about the target as much as it's about the bully. It is about their perceived slight or sense of injustice that sends them off. They use digital tools to make their target pay over and over again for whatever maltreatment they have done to the bully, real or inferred.

The following examples portray the myriad ways cyberbullies may make their targets feel pain.

1. Cyber Hacks

1.1 The World Cup attracted online cyberattackers as much as it attracted fans[1]

The cloud-based security service Incapsula was infiltrated by blackmail gaming providers that hid behind fake IP addresses. The attacks on over four vectors stemmed up to 24 hours. The bigger the event, the more primed blackmailing hackers are for penetrating the system to siphon off some of the betting.

1.2 Internet Billboards was hacked

In hiring a new chief technology officer, the curation firm Internet Bill-boards discovered a script in its website that was not supposed to be there. The previous security contractor missed the threat and it went undetected for about four months.

Founder Tom George was devastated. "Basically the script was sending out emails from my account, which as you can imagine without knowing the details of the emails sent, I find it very troubling."

The new security fellow eliminated the threat and the company committed to put more emphasis on security and preventing intruders from breaching the system.

Because he was not aware of the problem or its duration, and that nobody alerted him there was an issue, the firm was faced with restoring its digital imprint.

George discovered the company had been put on several blacklists. "We are a legitimate company and have nothing to hide. Now that we have resolved the issue, I've taken the necessary steps to ensure our

---

1 "World Cup Attracts Online Betting Cyber Attackers," Online-Casinos.com, accessed December, 2014. www.online-casinos.com/news/12860-world-cup-attracts-online-betting-cyber-attackers

good graces with Google and initiated the process of having us removed from any such lists."

1.3 Mobile infiltrations

Mobile hacking is a thing but it doesn't have to be your thing if you take some simple precautions. AccountingDegree.com lists 10 things to watch out for, so that you don't have to be some creep's next victim[2]:

1. Beware of root kit installations. These are software programs that install themselves. Make sure the apps you download are direct from the Apple Store or the Chrome Web Store/Google Play.

2. QR codes could take you for a ride. You don't really know where a QR code links to until it's been scanned. You might be going to a site that is laden with a virus or malware.

3. Digital certificates can be stolen. A certificate essentially verifies an identity. When you click on a bookmark, note the address that comes up in the bar. If it looks fishy, go directly to the website by typing in the direct address.

4. Don't let anyone smish you into private details. Smishers bait you into revealing personal information, and all of a sudden, your bank account and credit cards are empty. If you receive a text or email to confirm information, don't click the link. If you think it may be legitimate, type the address into the address bar and go direct to the website.

5. Social engineers do the same thing as smishers do. If you get an invoice with questionable charges; if anything suspicious or wrong information comes across your device, do not click any links. Type the proper address into the address bar and go directly to the site to log in.

6. We love free WiFi at our favorite coffee house and at the airport. However, it is insecure, and if you have to use it, know that someone inside or outside is lying in wait for you to log into your bank account and steal your password.

7. It doesn't matter what your device is, everyone is at risk from viruses and malware. Malware is that perpetual cold that turns into the flu and the virus is Ebola. Protect yourself with a recommended antivirus product.

---

2 "Mobile Commerce Crime: 10 Scary Trends to Watch Out For," AccountingDegree.com, accessed December, 2014. www.accountingdegree.com/blog/2012/mobile-commerce-crime-10-scary-trends-to-watch-out-for

8. When you purchase your device or download an app from an unverified dealer, you are putting yourself at risk for crimeware. You are not techie enough to notice, until it is too late, that someone secretly downloaded a spy program onto your device so they can defraud you.

9. Encryption is like having a Mac. You might think you are safe from all external threats, but there are a percentage of crawlies that creep through to steal your identity. That said, financial institutions implement more than just encryption programs to safeguard their consumers. There is more than one layer of protection. Where encryption infiltration might occur is through lack of proper safeguards and layers of security, which is what we saw in the Target hacking[3]. As the official reason for the breach has not been confirmed, it has been rumored that it came from a supplier's end - where they logged into the Target system from a compromised system.

10. Electronic eavesdropping is what happens on unsecured WiFi and malicious apps. It can also happen in your own home. Know where your mobile apps come from and use common sense on the Web. Secure your router.

2. Harassment

Cyberbullies use any digital media available to spread their wrath, even email. Emails are generally easy to trace, but it is difficult to prove if the owner of the account was actually the one to send the message. Fortunately there are email filters that allow you to block or filter such emails into the trash and report them for spam.

When a cyberbully creates a website or a web page to torment and harass, it is likely a violation of the local or regional Internet Service Provider's Terms of Use or Acceptable Use Policies. The ISP may have an email account where you can report the abuse. There is no guarantee you'll have success.

2.1 Fatal attraction, Internet-style

Move over Glenn Close, the Internet brings in a new wave of fatal attraction. Imagine receiving this from your ex: 77,000+ telephone

---

3 "Target says up to 70 million more customers were hit by December data breach," *The Washington Post*, accessed December, 2014. www.washingtonpost.com/business/economy/target-says-70-million-customers-were-hit-by-dec-data-breach-more-than-first-reported/2014/01/10/0ada1026-79fe-11e3-8963-b4b654bcc9b2_story.html

calls; 41,000+ text messages; and about 2,000 emails — all in the span of one week. Well, it didn't happen[4], but it sure is believable.

This was one of those fake stories coming from the World News Daily Report, which is really a satirical website. That said, it doesn't take much to get people to believe these days, so you have to know this story spread like wildfire.

Why it is so believable is because we all know of the date-gone-bad stories, where the person who called it off gets 100 texts a day. You're just glad when you hear about them that you're not one of them.

3. Internet Defamation
3.1 TTC runs red light then nearly kills woman

Admittedly, it was a very scary incident[5]. Sitting at a red light watching a bus pass through a red light and narrowly miss a pedestrian — all caught on camera — would unnerve the best of us.

What happens when we capture something amazing or life-changing? We post it to YouTube, almost immediately. We don't often think of the consequences of our post and how it might affect the people in the video, even if it appears they did something stupid and lawless.

Peer pressure and trolls in the comment feed often trigger a drastic response from the company to whom the person who made the mistake is beholden to. In the case of this video, the bus driver was fired without being interviewed. While it doesn't change the near-miss, by the time the driver noticed the red light, it was too late to stop and she swerved the bus to try and miss the pedestrian.

The videographer did not intend for the bus driver to be fired and regretted his post.

Anyone who has driven a larger vehicle knows you need more distance to stop. Everyone who drives should know that drivers make mistakes, even when they are not tired, distracted, or under the influence of a substance. The speed at which the digital universe operates, any post displaying full unadulterated guilt or one that is taken out of context is sure to be vilified by cyber trolls, no matter what the truth might be.

---

4   "Satirical story generates Internet buzz," krqe.com, accessed December, 2014. http://krqe.com/2014/06/30/satirical-story-generates-internet-buzz/?hpt=ju_bn3
5   "Posting TTC red light video was a mistake, says man who put it on YouTube," TheStar.com, accessed December, 2014. www.thestar.com/news/gta/2014/07/30/ttc_red_light_video_a_mistake_says_man_who_posted_it.html

3.2 Why Is Lambda Legal cyberbullying a small business?

When someone feels slighted, or feels that they've been discriminated against, they usually tell their friends. But this group took it a step further. They created a social media campaign to disparage a restaurant[6].

Bistro 18 Hookah Bar had been catering to a gay-friendly neighborhood in Washington, DC. Some of its staff was gay and it held events for the LGBT community, so intolerance was not in its business model. But on one occasion?, a transgender person and her friends claimed the restaurant, via one server, discriminated against them. So they tagged up with the Lambda Legal Transgender Rights Project Director and retaliated with a human rights complaint and by spreading the discrimination outrage across the Internet — even though the restaurant had fired the server in question.

Bistro 18 saw a large drop in its Yelp rating and on other sites, but most of the people writing the reviews were from outside the Washington area. The Lambda group showed no concern when asked about the restaurant's business suffering as a result.

4. Prohibited Creditor Practices

4.1 Debt collectors troll debtor's friends on Facebook

Even though you further your social media experience by connecting with people you don't initially know, it might be wise to vet their profiles before you click the "Accept" button. One of them could be a collections agent[7] hired by one of your creditors to troll your Facebook friends to find you and harass you.

This tactic violates the US's *Fair Debt Collections Practices Act* (FDCPA).

One debt collector sent a friend request pretending to be a woman in a bikini. The identity was finally revealed when the person wrote on his wall telling him to pay up, calling him a deadbeat.

A debt collector disclosed the debt to the consumer's other Facebook friends and also tried to get the consumer's Facebook friends to get him to contact the agency. The collector called the consumer several times a day and left numerous text messages. A neighbor was contacted and a letter was sent to the consumer's employer.

6 "Why Is Lambda Legal Cyberbullying a Small Business?," Bilerico.com, accessed December, 2014. www.bilerico.com/2014/06/why_is_lambda_legal_cyberbullying_a_small_business.php
7 "Why Can't We Be Friends?," FDCPA.me, accessed December, 2014. www.fdcpa.me/facebook-friends-debt-collector

9

The Law and Cyberbullying

The first thing a person must do when he or she learns they are the target of a cyberbully is find out where the post originated.

If it is a dedicated web page, you can use www.whois.net to find out who owns the domain. You can also find out through who.godaddy.com. The information will include server and hosting details, contact information of the owner, who the domain is registered through, the creation date, and the expiry date.

When it comes to a social media post, if it has been retweeted, and reposted several times, you'll need to find a way to trace it back to its origin.

Libel is so hard to prove. You need a defendant, and you can't go after any of the service providers or the social media sites themselves. Of course, you would go to Twitter, Tumblr, Facebook and other sites to ask to have the post removed. But after that, who do you go after?

I presented Hawkins with the scenario: a blogger posts a piece on Huffington Post, and in the comment feed, someone writes a highly salacious and libelous remark to disparage someone mentioned in the post. Her response was that the person who posted the comment would own the words.

However, she continues, "I don't think that would rise to the level of copyright. The question to ask is who is responsible for the words, and what is said? Does it incite? Creating a meme sometimes can be an issue of creating incitement, potentially under First Amendment right, and can be stopped. Law enforcement can force the ISP to block stuff. I don't know for certain if they use any legal grounds for it, according to terms of service, to start blocking stuff like that."

Hawkins affirms that you always own your words, whether they are copyrightable or not.

Then there is the story of Jada, a 16-year-old who attended a party, but her first drink was spiked and she woke up to discover naked pictures of her unconscious body had spread around the Internet accompanied by the hashtag #jadapose. Others took pictures of themselves in the same pose and spread them with the hashtag, mocking the fact that she had been raped[1].

On the Jada case, Hawkins replies, "We are looking at photos that are potentially in the commitment of a crime, and this is not a joke. Unfortunately, we really don't have laws regarding stuff like that."

Other than the US's First Amendment, there really isn't a federal definition. There are acts that fit into different crimes, but for most of the acts of cyberbullying, there is no federal legal scheme to prevent it in the United States. State laws are so delayed in social media that law enforcement doesn't even know where to start. So they don't do anything.

Because this is an area of law that Hawkins is working in, she admits it is a hard thing to specialize in. "That's why a number of lawyers are starting to trying to put together a special team for Internet crimes that go beyond simple cyberbullying. The problem is you can't go to your local law enforcement officer and invoke this federal law in their jurisdiction. They're left holding the book to see what their state does."

That is why you see the international activist and hacktivist network Anonymous become so powerful. They are tired of seeing victims

1   "#JadaPose: the online ridiculing of a teen victim is part of a sickening trend," TheGuardian.com, accessed December, 2014. www.theguardian.com/lifeandstyle/womens-blog/2014/jul/17/jadapose-online-ridiculing-rape-victims-sickening-trend

underserved and the known perpetrators see no consequence for their actions.

Corporations have consequences because there are laws related to what they can do. If they're hacking into systems and into private organizations, that is regulated by various federal agencies.

"It is always easier to go after a corporate defendant because they potentially have the bigger pocket and you can get lawyers who are willing to represent you if your case is strong enough. Chances are a corporation has, at minimum, policies in place their employees have to abide by. An employee violating a corporate policy, and then nothing being done, there is at least some claim for damages, even if it's basic negligence, which is the ultimate last step — going for basic negligence. As an individual, you don't have that safety net."

It can be frustrating until these laws evolve and catch up with the times. The police really don't know what to do, and that's usually the first place you go when something happens. If it's not something they see as stalking, in the traditional sense, then it might not even raise enough of a red flag, because they look at is as if there is no imminent threat.

One of the biggest misunderstandings of what cyberbullying, cyber extortion, cyber harassment, and cyber stalking is — because it's not somebody knocking at your door, physically following you in your car — there is no anticipated threat. You can shut off your computer and it seemingly goes away. But we all know that in reality, that's not how it works. You can get a new phone number, but the bullying, stalking, and harassment continues. Nobody knows how to stop it.

What the police will do with a physical threat is someone will stake out your house. If you tell them your ex-boyfriend is constantly coming to your house, and here are pictures, the police will send a car to watch for him and arrest him for trespassing.

What do you do when somebody is trespassing your cyber bubble? The police can't physically stake that out.

Phishing and hacking are covered under a number of federal laws. However, the majority of those who are phishing and hacking are not located in North America. So what do you do? You can't go after them. You can only hope that people are educated enough and that they take great lengths to educate their consumers. "We would never ask you these things. This is what our emails look like. If you have any questions, call us. Don't ever click on a link. We would never a link to ask for any identifying information."

When people are outside your jurisdiction, you don't have an ally. The police were not created to handle anything that is not physically experienced.

Hawkins maintains, "We have law enforcement trained in online pedophilia and in child pornography. Over time, we've seen these as vulnerable populations. We just have not caught up to the fact that people who are jerks in person are sometimes jerks online. We don't know how to draw that fine line. You have somebody posting a threat on Facebook because they're mad at something that is going on at Reddit, and they're in a Facebook Reddit group. They post in this group, 'You think I'm a wimp, wait until you see me blow up a school.' It is a threat to commit a crime. Yet at the same time, you've got stories like the Jada situation. There is no platform that says it's okay to post lewd photos of a child. If there is a question as to how old that person was, that photo should have been flagged immediately, as soon as it started going viral."

Then there is discussion about a post itself and who it offends. We see exceptions based on our polarized political climate in North America. For example, a hunter proudly posts a selfie with a big game animal he or she has just captured. Other hunters and hunting advocates will not be offended, and instead pat the hunter on the back for a job well done. Meanwhile, animal rights supporters may take offense to the post and think it is highly inappropriate for a public forum. These kinds of things add a slippery slope for lawmakers and law enforcement.

When it is something that really needs to be shut down and the laws are just not there yet to prosecute, if it doesn't fall into the current categories of justice, then all one can do is create awareness and lobby for change.

For the majority of the population, they might think that other people are taking care of it. In the case of cyberbullying in schools, the schools should take care of it. Even though 49 states (except Montana) have mandated a school cyberbullying policy, you still hear story after story about schools doing nothing to enforce it.

According to Hawkins, cyberbullying is a terroristic, extortion type of activity, yet there is no law that says it is particularly illegal.

Jeremy Pomeroy is the managing member at Pomeroy Law Group PLLC in New York City, specializing in media, technology, and intellectual property law. He notes, "The laws tend to hang their hats on the words of the traditional action."

Traditional laws: libel, defamation, stalking, and unfair competition are where some of these cyber-actions might fit in. The stalking and other laws might extend to online but it depends on how the statute is drafted. Some states may have enacted new cyberbullying laws, but federally, some of it would fall into the First Amendment.

When a post crosses the line, Pomeroy renders it a matter of business and state law if there is an element of libel or defamation.

"It might involve false statements that damage the reputation in some way. Statements of opinion aren't considered libelous. 'I went to the hotel and the room was full of bedbugs.' If that's not true, that would have to be a libelous comment."

These comments can be very damaging to a business. You yell it to the world and put it up on TripAdvisor.com or wherever a bad review would get the most impact, and it has the potential to be very destructive.

User-generated content, third party content, and comments are generally insulated from libel. If the speaker were anonymous, a subpoena would be needed, something that would not be readily easy to get.

There are circumstances where the publisher is actively responsible, if it is guiding or editing the content. It's a pretty broad limitation, however.

Pomeroy seconds what Hawkins said, "The third-party speaker you could go after if you could figure out who they are. Individuals tend to be untouchable."

The local laws are evolving, but the Internet makes everyone potentially a global publisher. So if you're the bully, you don't even know which law is going to govern your comment if it is published worldwide. It could be in Singapore.

Not surprising, there are some immunities, such as with politicians. Parliamentary or legislative immunity[2] offers partial immunity from the libelous comments you hear during election campaigns and throughout the course of governance. This law applies to several countries, including the United States and Canada.

2   "Parliamentary immunity," Wikipedia.org, accessed November, 2014.
    http://en.wikipedia.org/wiki/Parliamentary_immunity

The sharing and re-sharing of intellectual property makes it a difficult thing to take to court. Then there is the anonymity of some bullies.

Some litigation examples don't do much to instill confidence. Pomeroy cites one that happened years ago. A medical practice asked everyone to sign a standard form, which signed over copyright to anything published. A comment later showed up on a website and it was deemed to be unenforceable.

When employees breach the duty of loyalty by revealing trade secrets and other private information, the contractual obligation to protect confidentiality can be used to go after them.

Before a lawyer will seriously look at a case, it has to be strong. They do a cost-benefit analysis: if you do prevail, what's the gain? However, one could have a lawyer send a cease and desist letter instead.

"To accuse someone of fraud is a damaging statement," acknowledges Pomeroy, "and if you made it knowing it was untrue, or were careless about whether it was untrue, that would fall under the category of libel *per se*. It is the kind of thing that is so damaging that the damages are presumed."

Before you proceed, consider how strong your case is. What are your odds of prevailing? What's your objective? Even if you were good at prevailing, how much is it going to cost you to get to that end result? Think about the public relations aspect of it. Suing a bunch of individuals doesn't really play well in the press for a corporation. It may look like you have a personal issue.

Pomeroy puts forward that "commercial speech does not portray much protection under the First Amendment. Statements, opinion, and statements about your business is a matter of public interest. Those are things that the First Amendment is likely to protect. For example, the Sucks.com franchises for various company names, the owner of the sucks domain name has since prevailed on a trademark claim. Whether or not they are affiliated with the actual company, statements, and opinion, it's pretty hard to shut that down."

Fake sites have almost become a part of the Internet culture. When something happens, immediately someone grabs a Twitter handle to circulate humorous and ridiculous tweets to compound a company's mistake or bad public relations move. If a company succeeded in shutting one of them down, another would pop up almost immediately, and would probably include tweets about shutting down other sites.

There is no doubt, especially in Canada, that one will need very deep pockets if they choose to pursue a case of online harassment or cyber libel[3]. Even though "defamatory libel" is included in the Criminal Code of Canada, it is rarely charged. Police will encourage the target to seek justice is in civil court. It is rarely tackled because the outcome is uncertain and it can be an extremely lengthy and expensive process, which may unleash more dirty laundry to the public realm.

Brian Burke learned this firsthand in 2013[4], when he was general manager of the Toronto Maple Leafs. He wanted 18 anonymous commenters to be held responsible for their libelous words. He was accused of having an extramarital affair with a reporter with whom he was alleged to have fathered a child. It wasn't true.

The downside of his serving the injunction was it made the comments even more public than they were. If a hockey fan hadn't heard about or read the comments, they knew about them after the act of suing the authors hit the press.

His lobby for justice involved court orders to compel web hosts and Internet service providers to provide the information they had that would identify the defendants. In response to the suit, one of the authors, @THEzbrad, sent out a Tweet, "I think he's just angry that 'his' Toronto team finally made the playoffs. Sorry Burkey."

Burke has continued pursuit of his tormentors. In September 2013, he successfully secured a default judgment in the BC Supreme Court to serve to the commenters on the same message board they defamed him on. He was still investigating their identities.

1. Legislation to End Anonymity on the Internet

In 2012, the New York Assembly and Senate looked to initiate the Internet Protection Act[5], a move to stop anonymous trolls from cyberbullying the online community.

The bill reads: "Anonymous postings on the Internet not only can harm the persons or businesses being directly victimized, but they also hurt the public in general. When anonymous posters hide behind the

---

3   "Online defamation cases often unrealistic for Canadians: Expert," GlobalNews.ca, accessed November, 2014. http://globalnews.ca/news/674540/online-defamation-cases-often-unrealistic-for-canadians-expert

4   "Brian Burke cyber-libel suit a reminder anonymous Internet commentators can be unmasked," TheStar.com, accessed December, 2014. www.thestar.com/news/gta/2013/04/27/brian_burke_cyberlibel_suit_a_reminder_anonymous_internet_commentators_can_be_unmasked.html

5   "How to Better Fight Cyberbullying: Finding Fixes for the Internet Protection Act," Verdict.justia.com, accessed December, 2014. http://verdict.justia.com/2012/06/01/how-to-better-fight-cyberbullying

Internet to facilitate a crime (such as harassment) or as a vehicle for defamation, innocent men, women, and children are openly victimized, and the public is intentionally mislead. ... This legislation simply provides a means for the victim of an anonymous posting on a website to request that such a post be removed, unless the anonymous poster is willing to attach his or her name to it."

This sounds pretty good in theory, but there are plenty of cyberbullies who do attach their names to their posts. You can also see how the wording of this legislation might scream a violation of the First Amendment.

There are other laws that allow someone to get a protective order for stalking and harassment. Not all anonymous Internet users are threatening or abusive.

Passing a cyberbullying law does have a conflict with the First Amendment. Let's take the abortion issue as an example. Someone could post an article on a Facebook page in support of abortion rights. The comment feed will begin to fill with mirroring voices, but there will be some opposition, and one or two of them will vehemently state their case using vile and inciting language, while posting a horrific picture of a dead fetus or worse. An argument ensues in the feed and the temperature of the posts from both sides of the discussion grows stronger.

Where the First Amendment and freedom of speech (under the Canadian Charter of Rights and Freedoms) would come in is that the person who owns the original post and some of his or her friends will be highly offended by the person in opposition and the way they voiced their opinion. Some might even consider the response to be bullying, especially if the conversation continues. The person in opposition might consider the original post as highly offensive and is trying to call that person out and let them know just how offensive it is. As a way to pay someone back for their adverse opinion, the post, or the comment, might be reported to the website owner as spam and abusive. But in reality, whether you like someone's opinion or not, each has the right to share it. Commenters may or may not be using their own names.

How the Internet is set up, anyone can set up a website, email account, or social media without using their own name. Even if a driver's license or passport is required to open up an account (and it is not), there are plenty of individuals who can put you in touch with someone who can provide fake documents.

This is a difficult legislation to pass without giving up rights in other areas, when there are already harassment and defamation laws. Going back to the abortion post example, none of that vitriol would qualify for this legislation.

2. Debt Collection Laws

2.1 My story

I've been working freelance contract work, specializing in writing and publishing since I formed my proprietorship company in 1990. (I've been incorporated since 2011.) In essence, I'm a self-employed entrepreneur.

Like most small businesses, my financial chart has zig-zagged up and down. The ups are fantastic. The downs are catastrophic. Adding to that normal ebb and flow were two incidents that resulted in severe financial setbacks:

1. I was hit by a car as a pedestrian in 2001.

2. I severed the anterior cruciate ligament (ACL) in my right knee, playing lacrosse with the Calgary Roughnecks in 2005.

At the start of 2008, I began working with a book client who was located in another province. He was someone I was really excited about working with, but he wasn't an easy client; however he wasn't the worst. I agreed to undercharge him, thinking that the project would not be as big a job as some of my others. Of course, it ended up being as much work as the bigger jobs, still, I did not revisit the quote. It was a fee-for-service contract.

When the project was completed, the client was satisfied with the end result. His input was needed at every step and nothing moved forward without his okay.

The client was unable to directly sell his product because it would have put him in a conflict of interest position with his licensed business. So he asked me to do the fulfilment for him. He also subcontracted one of my associates to help him with marketing it worldwide. The marketing was a fee-for-service contract between him and the associate. The fulfilment was based on a percentage, which ended up breaking even, and in some cases, it cost me money when an international or United States buyer clicked the Canadian shipping rates. I did this task from 2008 to 2012.

Until near the end of 2009, business was so good, I was working about 10 projects a month, and then about October, I realized all the projects I was working on were existing jobs. No new projects were coming in.

Publishing took a big hit with the recession, coupled with the fact the industry was changing. I had a full-time assistant I had to let go. I kept her three months too long but my guilt kept delaying the process and her salary really helped put me behind.

I went from making $10,000 a month to less than $1,000. I had to reinvent my business, because publishing projects were just not coming in as everyone was feeling the pinch. Plus the digital world was blossoming, and I had to find a way to try and find the formula to stay ahead of the curve. Meanwhile, I had to also find another form of work. It was tough. The recession laid off a lot of people and when you're over 50, there are even fewer options. I certainly was not alone.

There were many trips needed to the post office for this client's fulfilment, and while I did struggle to get the books out, accounting was sporadic because I would run out of time after taking care of a few other book projects on top of the agency job. Still, this client did still receive his fulfilment checks. He wasn't too keen on them being off schedule, but I was doing the best I could. When he first gave me grief, I should have stopped and shipped all his books back to him then, but I didn't.

The other job I had found didn't need me anymore and I was back to square one. I was getting paid for a few workshops and had a couple of projects, but it really wasn't a lot. On about three occasions, a client would pay me on the 5th when the rent was due on the 1st and my landlords were unrelenting and would give me an eviction notice on the second, then charge me interest when I paid them on the 5th or the 7th (depending on where the weekend was). That was stressful and gave me some sleepless nights.

I was too proud to tell anyone my predicament. Like most entrepreneurs, I did not want anyone to know, because many in my community seemed to look to me to lift them up. I was supposed to be the one helping them to follow their dreams.

I still had a lot of bills from 2009 that had almost all had gone to collections. I worked with all of them and tried to put something on the accounts when I could, no matter how minimal. They could at least see I was trying.

In the summer, after receiving a payment, this client, tired of the funds not showing up like clockwork every month (I would send a few months at a time when I was able to get to the accounting), got his lawyer to send me a demand letter. Well, that changed everything. Immediately, I dropped everything, and as you are supposed to do, I stopped communicating with the client and only spoke with the lawyer, via email. At that point, I immediately loaded every last remnant of his project and bussed it to the lawyer's office with an inventory and accounting of what I assessed I owed. I got every last trace of toxic energy out of my house.

Eventually, I decided to give up the house I was renting and head to the place where this new business venture would eventually take place. I sold my car to my neighbor; gave every last stick of furniture, bedding, household goods, even most of my clothes to the homeless shelter (they backed a truck onto the front lawn and took it all); and with the help of a wonderful friend, I was able to find the money to travel and sustain myself in the new location for a while. I felt I needed to do it for my own sanity and to familiarize myself with the place I wanted to end up in. Plus we also thought a new project I was working toward might come through during the time I was there.

So I left in my wake a string of bills, including this client's fulfilment. I had sent a check to him (via his lawyer) in August and I left in September. In my communications with the lawyer, I never said I wouldn't make good and I innocently kept in contact with them periodically afterwards. I received no reply.

The clock turned 2013 and I still heard nothing from the lawyer since my last communication, which might have been in November 2012. I still wasn't in a position to do anything but my intention was to take care of it when I could.

I was looking for contract work. That February, I did find a couple jobs that seemed to be confirmed, where I just had to wait for the delivery of the contract. But then nothing happened. Silence. How rude, I thought.

It seemed like getting new business was at a dead end. Meanwhile, there were a couple really small jobs that brought in $300 here and there — basically covering food and not really a lot of shelter. I was actually being helped and housed by friends and family. At no fixed address, outside of the Internet, I was technically homeless and as good as stranded in another country.

It was about six months after I had last contacted this client's lawyer, now staying with a family member, and I noticed a post online that accused me of fraud. It was a dedicated web page this client had created on his website. Now it made sense why there was no new business! The post also said there was a judgment. I was not in receipt of any judgment. It also said I had flown the country, had never communicated, and was not able to be found. Apparently this man's lawyer did not communicate with his client.

I finally received an email from the client's lawyer in May, something like 40 days after I saw the web post. Accompanying the email was a Notice of Judgment. It was not dated anywhere near those prior months or when the web post was estimated to have been created. The amount on the document was also more than double of what the actual accounting showed when I returned the remaining inventory.

Then I got angry.

I emailed the lawyer and said I was disputing the judgment. Before my documentation had an opportunity to reach the court, I received the actual judgment. It was fast-tracked once they received my acknowledgment. Adding insult to injury, the court told me I had to file the dispute in person. So it was all right for me to be served electronically, but I was not able to dispute it electronically. We were on opposite sides of the country.

With the advice of a friend, I went on the offensive. I screenshot everything, dug away at Google to find anything else this cyberbully of a client was posting. Sure enough, I found Facebook and Twitter posts. I made sure to take a screenshot of the post and all the comments associated with it. In the Facebook post, one of the client's followers wrote that he would send an email of a fake job offer. The client wrote that he should be careful and not do anything that would get him in trouble, but he also wrote that it was his intention to ensure that my business would suffer. He wasn't interested in being paid. Screenshot! Then I blocked all of their sorry asses. I threw every last remnant of the client, the screenshots, and communications into an Excrement file that I loaded up to Google Drive and buried in another folder so that I would not be able to see it until I looked for it. I didn't want his toxic trash on my precious computer.

Then I called the police. After researching collection laws, libel, and cyberbullying laws, I learned that the client's dedicated web page was a violation of all of them. I had statutes, screenshots, and paperwork that included the client's ISP, his website details, and even that letter that put him in a conflict with his business license should he do something to disparage the integrity of his office.

Of course, what I've learned in doing the research for this book is that Internet crimes are new and police forces do not know how to handle them. What also had to happen was the local police would have to agree to forward the file to the police force in the client's jurisdiction. They weren't able to follow through but they did tell me I could use the police file number to file a libel case, which they said was a strong one — but it would have to be filed in the client's jurisdiction. There was a two-year statute of limitations.

I had many legal options, as you will see in the following sections where I'll cover laws that are available to prosecute under.

There was no doubt I was ready to find a kick-ass lawyer specializing in cyber libel. I won't always be broke no matter how long that post stays front and center on Google, even if it's for the next 50 years. But as we all know, court cases can take years. The only people who really benefit are the lawyers, even if you win. The time commitment, the stress, the he-said/she-said, the dirty laundry — you have to weigh it to decide if it is worth taking that much of a chunk out of your life to pursue it. Plus the fact, you're practically married to the troll for all that time and there is no guarantee the post will come down. In fact, the publicity would probably add more posts.

The other thing to note is that the client's product, in its physical form, is not his under this country's copyright laws. My company actually owns the copyright to the creative of this project. I could implement an injunction to keep him from recreating future copies of it. He owns the manuscript, but I own the creation in final form. In our service contract, the wording said he owned 100 percent rights to the manuscript, not 100 percent exclusive rights, which include the layout and images. There wasn't a substantive edit, so the edited version of the manuscript would still be his. If he reprinted the project in its current form, he is in violation of copyright infringement. Add that to the list of charges.

I had some great advice given to me by my webcasting partner, so that is the advice I chose to follow. Instead of spending toxic energy to fight back through the justice system, I chose to write about it instead. This way, I hope to help others who have and will go through the same trauma.

This is really the first time I have made this story public. We all make mistakes. We are all human. I am especially human. We are all fragile beings, too, especially self-employed entrepreneurs.

You can judge me harshly and join this client's bandwagon. Those who are persecuted are in good company.

Use this book and this story to empower your own troubles. This is meant to be a step-by-step guide for you or someone you know who is going through it. You can't believe everything you see on the Internet.

I, for one, have learned a strong lesson, and I suppose I can thank my cyberbullying client for that. I now know not to judge others when I see a disparaging post online. After hearing about a lot more stories, I tend to now look at such posts as being untrue first.

I know I have been a bully myself online. I've said some nasty things. I've hurt a couple of people. I couldn't be sorrier, now that I know what it feels like. This has changed me for the good. I will no longer engage in toxic talk or allow it on any of my networks. I plan to use the Internet for good and only put stuff out there that inspires, educates, and entertains.

So when you see something written about anyone that is in a certain mode, consider the words of David Meerman Scott: "You are what you publish."

2.2 Is there a debtor's prison?

If you are in debt, the good news is there is no debtor's prison, but there are collectors and creditors who try to put you in prison through incessant calls, threats, and cyberbullying tactics. Many of these are in violation of the debt collection laws, which are on the books both federally and provincially and through each state (the laws are similar in both Canada and the United States).

You only need to turn on your television to see how stable (or rather, not) the economy has been since 2009. Recovery has been better in some centers, but that doesn't mean all of a sudden everyone is on Easy Street.

In fact, the average personal debt in Canada is over $100,000[6].

No wonder the collections industry is on the rise. Those companies seem to have enjoyed a healthy incline at the expense of others' misfortune.

It may be easy to judge those who have fallen into the credit abyss, but most people are just one paycheck away from the homeless shelter. An injury, industry downslide, job loss, health issue, natural disaster — anything can turn even the most financially secure to Collectionville.

If you are in collections and bearing through excessive, harassing telephone calls, or have discovered that your creditor is posting your said debt all over the Internet and trolling your Facebook and LinkedIn connections, check online for "debt collection violations" in your jurisdiction. If it is a collections agency doing the deed, there's a good chance you can cite the violation to the person acting it out and stop the behavior right there. If not, there are reporting options.

Let's take a look at the collections laws and prohibited creditor practices. Most of the rules apply both sides of the border and from state to state, province to province. There may be additional statutes listed in specific jurisdictions, so Google "debt collection laws" or "prohibited creditor practices" in your area.

2.3 Statutes of limitations

2.3a Statute of limitations on debt in the United States

Six years after the last recognition of a general debt, it is then deemed uncollectible or can be permanently written off. The limitation on legal files and any extensions will vary from state to state and depend on the type of debt.

2.3b Statute of limitations on debt in Canada

The debt is written off after six years after the last recognition of the debt and the account can no longer be sued.

For litigation in Alberta and Ontario, the limitation is two years after last recognition of the debt. The debt can still be reported on the debtors' credit bureau but the account can't be sued. The limitation

---

6 "Canadian Household Debt," HuffingtonPost.ca, accessed December, 2014.
   www.huffingtonpost.ca/news/canadian-household-debt

on legal files can spread to 10 years. It can be renewed for another 10 years in some circumstances.

Only a first party lender, debt buyer, lawyer, or licensed collection agency can collect money in Canada.

Know your rights.

2.4 United States collections

Violations of the US Fair Debt Collections Practices Act (FDCPA):

- Collectors are harassing a debtor by communicating through Facebook accounts.

- A collector that requests to become a Facebook friend and fails to disclose to the consumer that it is attempting to collect a debt or the identity of their collection agency.

- A collector disclosing the debt to the Facebook user's other friends, virtual or otherwise.

Unfair Debt Collection Practices under the Federal Trade Commission[7]:

- The collector cannot contact the debtor's family, friends, employers, or any other person about the debt.

- The collector cannot engage in name-calling.

- Threats of criminal prosecution, physical violence, and cyber stalking are prohibited.

- The collector can only speak with an employer if confirming or correcting location information about the consumer. They must not disclose the debt and cannot communicate with the same person again unless requested to do so to correct erroneous and incomplete information that was given.

- The collector cannot communicate by postcard.

- The collector cannot use language or a symbol on an envelope or in the contents of any other communications via mail or telegram that denotes the sender is a debt collector or that it relates to debt collection.

- A collector may not harass, oppress, or abuse the debtor.

---

7 "Debt Collection," FTC.gov, accessed December, 2014.
   https://www.consumer.ftc.gov/articles/0149-debt-collection

- A collector may not threaten the reputation or property of the debtor.

- A collector may not publish a list of consumers that owe money, even if they allegedly refuse [Section 603(f) or 604(3) of the Act].

- The collector may not advertise the sale of debt to coerce payment.

- The collector may not continuously call or engage the debtor, or any person at the same location, on the telephone with the intent to abuse or harass.

- The collector must identify themselves in any communications and not use false and deceptive measures to collect the debt or obtain information about the consumer.

- The collector must not contact a consumer if he or she is represented by a lawyer.

- The collector must not represent what the debtor owes (such as inflating the amount and adding unreasonable interest fees).

- The collector must not tell the consumer they have sent legal paperwork when they have not.

Note: In 2010, 30 million Americans dealt with medical collections that were already paid, while the debt collectors would not remove the inaccurate information from the consumer's credit report. As a result, consumers were denied loans and were faced with paying high interest rates on credit cards and other loans.

You have one year from the date the law was violated to sue a collector in a state or federal court. A win means the judge can make the collector pay damages if you can prove lost wages and medical bills, etc. Even if you can't prove suffering, the collector can be ordered to pay up to $1,000. You would also be reimbursed for lawyer's fees and court costs. A class-action lawsuit of more than one consumer could recover up to $500,000 or one percent of the collector's net worth (whichever is lower). However, the original debt is still owed.

2.5 Collections in Canada

We won't get into every province because many of the statutes are similar across the country. There may be some slight differences, but when it comes to prohibited practices, there is unison on the types of behavior that are frowned upon.

Ontario amended the *Collection Agencies Act* and other acts in 2013 to update the term "collection agency" and "collector." A "collection agency" means:

- A person, other than a collector, who obtains or arranges for payment of money owing to another person or who holds one-self out to the public as providing such a service.

- A person, other than a collector, who provides debt settlement services.

In Ontario, Canada, a collection agency or collector may not:

- Collect additional funds than the said debt at the time it was sent to collections.

- Contact anyone else related to the said debt.

- Publish or threaten to publish the debtor's failure to pay.

- Communicate in such a manner or with such frequency as to constitute harassment.

- From the *Collection and Debt Settlement Services Act*[8], R.S.O. 1990, Chapter C.14: "Collectors are prohibited from falsifying information or documents, or getting someone else to contravene by doctoring information or assisting the agency in its deceptive behavior under the Debt Settlement Services Agreement."

Did you know that a collection agency must send you a written notice through the mail, and this notice must include: the name of the person or business that says you owe them money; the amount you owe; the name of the collection agency. Then it has to wait six days before contacting you.

Collection agents are not allowed to contact you more than three times in a seven-day period without your consent.

It doesn't count as a contact when you haven't answered their phone call or email and if they left a voice message.

A collector is not allowed to contact you on statutory holidays, on Sundays except between 1:00 p.m. and 5:00 p.m., and can only contact you on other days between 7:00 a.m. and 9:00 p.m.

8 *Collection Agencies Act*, Government of Ontario, accessed December, 2014. www.e-laws.gov.on.ca/html/statutes/english/elaws_statutes_90c14_e.htm

Collectors are not allowed to threaten, swear, or intimidate you and use excessive pressure in their pursuit of the said debt.

Unless your employer has guaranteed the debt, collectors are not allowed to contact them, unless it is with respect to a court order or wage garnishee or you have provided written authorization.

2.6 If you've been taken to collections or had to file for bankruptcy, you're in good company

Here are a few names you might have heard of[9] who have been through their own share of financial grief[10].

2.6a Abraham Lincoln

He went from job to job as a younger man. When he filed for bankruptcy, creditors took his horse and surveying gear, which were his only assets and it was not enough to cover the debt. He was making payments until the 1840s.

2.6b Henry Ford

He was faced with bankruptcy in 1901 when his automobile plant could only produce 20 vehicles. The firm reorganized into the Henry Ford Company, although he left it and founded a new company in 1903: the Ford Motor Company.

2.6c Milton Hershey

Hershey struggled selling sweets in New York City after his store went bankrupt. He was able to reorganize and discovered the process of using fresh milk in caramel production. Next, he formed the Lancaster Caramel Company in Pennsylvania.

2.6d Walt Disney

Disney formed the Laugh-O-Gram Studios out of Kansas City, which produced animated fairytales for the local theaters. While the product was popular, the firm Disney partnered with for financial backing went under, causing Disney's firm to file for bankruptcy.

2.6e Willie Nelson

Nelson had put his money into an illegal tax shelter, which resulted in the Internal Revenue Service seizing his assets in 1990 to cover his

9   "7 Wildly Successful People Who Survived Bankruptcy," MentalFloss.com, accessed December, 2014.
      http://mentalfloss.com/article/20169/7-wildly-successful-people-who-survived-bankruptcy
10 "Top 9 Celebrity Bankruptcies," TIME, accessed December, 2014.
      http://business.time.com/2012/02/16/top-9-celebrity-bankruptcies/slide/walt-disney-3

$16.7 million tax bill. Ironically, a compilation album *The IRS Tapes: Who'll Buy My Memories?* gave him the revenue he needed to settle the debt.

3. Criminal and Civil Codes and Laws

3.1 Cyberbullying and the law

Cyberbullying can be considered a criminal act or fall under civil law, but there are few actual statutes that are named with term cyberbullying. Instead, some of these crimes will fall under the code of harassment, civil rights, libel, and the First Amendment.

3.1a Canada

When you communicate with someone to the point that they fear their own safety, it falls under the Criminal Code of Canada. So does publishing defamatory libelous statement in a physical or digital medium that is intent on hurting another person's reputation. Spreading hate or discrimination based on race, national/ethnic origin, skin color, religion, age, sex, sexual orientation, marital status, family status, and disability is a violation of the Canadian *Human Rights Act*.

Each province and territory has its description as to what a bully or cyberbully is, but direct cyberbullying laws are only in reference to schools and students.

The Royal Canadian Mounted Police classify these as computer-assisted crimes[11].

- Invasion of privacy (which falls under Section 183 of the Criminal Code of Canada).

- Illicit collection, storage, modification, disclosure, transmission of personal data.

- Cyber espionage.

The Criminal Code of Canada defines cybercrime[12] as when someone uses a computer for hacking, phishing, spamming, child pornography, hate crimes, and computer fraud.

Harassment is when the bully says or does something to make the target fear for their safety or for the safety of others. Whether or not

---

11 "Integrated Technological Crime Unit," Royal Canadian Mounted Police, accessed December, 2014.
www.rcmp-grc.gc.ca/on/prog-serv/itcu-gict-eng.htm
12 "Cybercrime," Foreign Affairs, Trade and Development Canada, accessed December, 2014.
www.international.gc.ca/crime/cyber_crime-criminalite.aspx

the bully intended to frighten the personal safety of the target, they can still be charged.

Under law, cyber harassment and bullying targets can apply for a protection order against the said offender. The perpetrator faces a fine or up to five years in jail if they are found guilty of disobeying the order.

Criminal harassment convictions can mean prison time up to 10 years.

In Canada, libel is broken down[13] into two categories: Blasphemous and defamatory[14].

Before a charge is made in this area, it is determined whether what was said was fact or fiction. If the words are expressed in good faith and in acceptable language, or if it is just to poise a good argument in good faith, such as a political opinion, then it is not classified as libel.

What would fall under this section of the law is something like hate speech, where language is used to insult and inflame.

This is an indictable offense that can lead to up to two years in prison.

Defamatory libel includes anything that is published, without justification or excuse, with the intention of injuring a person's reputation and exposing them to hatred, contempt, and ridicule.

The libelous statement can be insinuated, or said in irony. It can be an image or another object that signifies libel. It is considered an act of libel when the act is made public, if anyone can see or read it, and if it is delivered in a way to cause someone to see or read it, other than the person it defames.

A conviction of defamatory libel can lead to imprisonment of up to five years.

In Ontario, *Libel and Slander Act* R.S.O. 1990, CHAPTER L.12, outlaws the spread of defamatory comments, spoken or written, that will affect a professional or business reputation. The plaintiff doesn't need to prove special damage if the words are crafted with intent to disparage an office, profession, calling, trade or business.

According to this law, if the publishing of libel and broadcast of slander is done through the Internet, the court does not see subsequent

---

13 Criminal Code (R.S.C., 1985, c. C-46), Government of Canada, accessed December, 2014.
   http://laws-lois.justice.gc.ca/eng/acts/C-46/index.html
14 "Blasphemous libel," Wikipedia.org, accessed December, 2014.
   http://en.wikipedia.org/wiki/Blasphemous_libel

shares of the hyperlink as a publication. Only the initial post would be in question. However, while the hyperlinks are considered content-neutral, they do reference the existence of the original post.

A comment only falls under free speech if:

- It is a matter of public interest.
- It is a fact.
- It includes inferences of fact but is recognized as a comment.
- If anyone might be able to utter the same opinion based on the proved facts (called an objective test).
- Even if the comment passes the objective test, the expression was proved to be actuated by malice[15].

The bottom line when proving libel or slander is: Can the average person off the street come up with the same conclusion or honest belief if he or she were presented with the facts?

The Supreme Court of Canada says malice is showing a blatant disregard for the truth when perpetration a libelous statement.

Injurious falsehood[16] or trade libel is the malicious publishing of false statements that incites a third party to act in a manner that causes actual harm, loss, or expense to the target. A common claim under this tort is damage to property, disparaging a product or business, thus affecting it marketability. The target has to prove the statements are false, that there was economic loss, and that the person acted maliciously and intended to cause injury with blatant disregard.

3.1b United States

There are federal statutes and each state has its own set of laws.

Defamation: Slander also falls under this category. Slander is auditory; libel is published. When a statement is made to imply something as fact in order to disparage an individual, business, product, group government or nation, this will fall under defamation.

Federally, this law is closely aligned with the First Amendment. Opinion is not defamation, so there must be a very strong case involving public concern. However, false statements of fact that hurt the

---

15 *Kim v. Dongpo News*, CANLII.org, accessed December, 2014. www.canlii.org/en/on/onsc/doc/2013/2013onsc4426/2013onsc4426.html?searchUrlHash=AAAAAQAOMjAxMyBPTlNDIDQ0MjYAAAAAAQ
16 "Injurious falsehood," McConchie Law Corporation, accessed December, 2014. www.libelandprivacy.com/areasofpractice_injuriousfalsehood.html

honor of an individual or business are not protected in the free speech provisions.

The Communications Decency Act absolves Internet service providers from accountability, regardless of what their users put online.

Actual malice: A public figure has to prove "actual malice" to push a defamation case forward. The perpetrator has to knowingly print or speak a false statement with reckless disregard for the truth.

Defamation *per se*: The target does not have to prove actual injury to their reputation in this case because it is presumed the harmful statements were defamatory.

Defamation *per quod*: Even though it would appear the defamation was harmful to the target, the target still has to prove the actual damages.

Single-publication rule: Even though a statement might be spread to other platforms online, if it is the same original statement, there is only one action for libel. This is similar to the Canadian law that sees a hyperlink as content-neutral.

10

Documenting Your Case

When you take the steps to document these ugly posts, it helps you begin to look at the event more objectively. You're building evidence for a case file, whether you decide to pursue justice or not. The more documentation you can muster for a police report, the more you control the case.

It is imperative you document in the early stages, at the time or right after you found the posts, just in case (and it would be a GREAT problem to have) the posts disappear.

You need a paper trail of the abuse. If it is warranted, you can also solicit statements from other people who have witnessed it and can testify objectively that they know the statements to be untrue. They can only speak to facts they can prove and their personal observations, not hearsay. These statements need to be dated and signed.

1. Take a Screenshot

If you are using a desktop, the button shown in Sample 2 is your new best friend. It is what you need to take a screenshot.

Sample 2
PrtScrn Button

Click this button, open up a Word document, and paste the image on the page.

There are a few ways you can paste.

1. Ctrl + c

2. Right-click on your mouse

3. Go to the top of the Word document and under the Home tab, click paste

If you don't have this button on your device, then Google: "how do I take a screenshot on Samsung Chromebook" or iPad, iPhone, Toshiba laptop, etc.

The beauty of the screenshot is it captures all the margins, including the time and date the screenshot was taken.

Sample 3 is a screenshot of my Pinterest boards taken from my desktop. Notice the address shows up at the top and at the bottom corner is the time and date of when I took the screenshot. This is a legal document. Screenshots are time-stamped from your computer. In general, images include information in its properties that tells you when it was taken, by what device, and if it was altered.

Sample 3
Pinterest Screenshot

2. Do a Forensic Audit

Depending on your popularity as a target and the reach of the original post, this could take a while.

When you go into Google, search under your name first, then search under any aliases you might use, such as Deb instead of Debbie, your company name, and other entities that are synonymous with you.

Check every page, including the ones that have been archived by Google. At the top of Google once the search results come up, check the tabs: Web, Images, Videos, News, and Books. Click onto the Search Tools button to open up the results if the default is too narrow (for example local).

If you find something linking you to the cyberbully, take a screenshot. Paste it into a running Word document and also paste in the URL. Do this for every post you find.

It is likely the cyberbully also used social media to spread the message against you. It may not always show up in Google. Break down every social media page you are on: Facebook, Twitter, LinkedIn, You-Tube, Google Plus, Tumblr. Use the search function the same as you did with Google: first your name, then any aliases you are known by, and your company — alone and linked with the cyberbully's name and aliases. Take more screenshots.

Make note of the people who participate in the cyber post in all of the venues. If there is a conversation under the post in social media, take a screenshot of the entire conversation. Write down the names of those who participated. See if any of them have furthered the posts through shares.

Don't block anyone until you are convinced there are no new posts circulating from that person. You won't be able to see what they share after you block them. Once you are satisfied you have all you can find, block their sorry asses into oblivion, including the names of those who participated in the feeds.

Keep an organized file of your screenshots and anything else you subsequently find. Back it up on your device and on the web (i.e. Google Drive). Put this file in a place where you can't view it and call it something like Excrement. Don't name your troll and don't let this folder hit your eyesight when you go into your device. Hide the folder in another folder (such as Personal). Keep it out of your view and your subconscious.

If your cyberbully has taken the time and energy to dedicate a web page to you, go through it line by line. For each line you can debunk, do that in a document. Save the document and put it in an Excrement file as I mentioned in the last chapter.

If there are harassment emails, save these as PDFs — the entire email — and add them to your Excrement file. Include the full header on the email and the entire feed of conversation, which will include forwards and replies. You can also report the abuse to your ISP.

Go to http://who.godaddy.com/ or http://whois.net/ to find out who owns the website your cyberbully has dedicated a web page to if it is not a social media site. See if the host (only if it is not your cyberbully — do not engage him/her) will remove the post (it's unlikely, but ask anyway). Copy and paste that information in another Word document and save it to the Excrement file.

Research your country/state/province as to the cyberbullying and cyber-libel laws. Copy and paste the highlights that apply to your situation, along with the source, in another document and save that to the Excrement file.

Now you are ready to file a police report. Yes, a police report. Even if your district police have never heard of cyberbullying, get it on record that this is NOT okay. Keep your police report and file number in a folder you can't see. Also scan it and put in the online Excrement file. Whether you pursue the police case or not, just having that file number will help with your recovery.

You may have to do some research to make sure you're filing in the correct jurisdiction. For example, is this going to be a federal case? Then you contact the federal authorities. They may still ask you to file with the local police.

Have copies of all your screenshots, including the ownership of the website, the name and address of your cyberbully if you have it, that person's ISP (that is also easy to find on Google if you have the email address and it will probably be in the website information).

3. To Sue or Not to Sue

After going through this process of documentation, you will now be ready for any criminal action the police might take, and also for a civil case.

If the case ends up being a civil one, you have a heady decision to make. Weigh the pros and cons of following through.

- Do you have the funds to pursue it? If not, can you find the funds?

- Is the case strong enough to take to court? Are you having trouble finding a lawyer?

- Will you have to relocate to where the case has to be filed? If the cyberbully is in another state or province, can you live with that inconvenience?

- Are you even able to sue the perpetrator? Do they live in another country?

- Is suing going to guarantee the posts get taken down?

- Are you prepared to be married to the cyberbully for as long as the court case will take - sometimes years?

- Will the court case generate more dirty laundry (on both sides) which will undoubtedly become public? Can you live with that?

- Are you physically and mentally strong enough to pursue the court case and receive all the ugliness it will generate?

- What if you lose?

Sometimes it is worth the risk and other times it may not be. Only you can decide. Take some time and solicit legal advice from a lawyer that specializes in this type of case.

In order to report cyberbullying with the authorities, use this checklist to gather the information they will require to build a case. The one thing cyberbullies are good at is leaving a paper trail.

- Screenshot documentation of the cyberbullying offenses, include the URL and the time you found them.

- Screenshot documentation of the website ownership of where the offenses occur.

- Email ISP information.

- A list of laws you think the cyberbully has broken (state/province and/or federal).

- Contact details of the cyberbully: email address, physical address, place of work, phone numbers, and any other pertinent information that would help with the case.

- Copies of harassment emails with the full email header, which will have date and time they were received.

- Screenshots of the offending group or community discussion, include the URL, profiles and emails of the offending person.

- Screenshots of the offending posts from social media sites, include the URL of the page and profile, name of the person, email address, screenshot of profile, date you saw the post.

- Screenshots of offending comments from chat rooms, include date and time of the chat, URL, name and email of the offending person, and screenshot of their profile.

11

Keyboard Cowards and Cyber Heroes: Examples of Business Cyberbullying

1. Keyboard Cowards

1.1 Robert Campbell of Ottawa: 181 charges of cyberbullying

A 42-year-old man from Ottawa, Ontario spent at least 12 years terrorizing 38 people through the Internet[1] in three countries. Robert Campbell was finally apprehended in 2014 and charged with 181 counts that included criminal harassment (27), identity fraud (69), and defamatory libel (85).

Campbell masked his identity online with elaborate software. His activity of cyberbullying and harassment desecrated lives and reputations of adults and children.

---

[1] "Ottawa man faces 181 charges related to cyberbullying, harassment," OttawaCitizen.com, accessed November, 2014. http://ottawacitizen.com/news/local-news/ottawa-man-faces-181-charges-for-international-cyberbullying-harassment

- He blackened the reputation of his own coworkers, sending out emails to spread rumors that there were allegations of alcohol abuse and unnatural sexual fetishes.

- He created a letter campaign to smudge victims as supporters of the Nazi party and as pedophiles.

- He set up fake profiles for his prey, showing them as gay, exotic dancers, Nazis, and called them disparaging names.

- He used email to make up stories about targets' health and in a target's name he invited random people to sex parties.

A collaborative effort among international law enforcement brought Campbell down.

1.2 Jesse Ventura wins $1.8 million in defamation case

Author Chris Kyle wrote in his book *American Sniper* that he hit a man in a California bar fight[2], who he identified as Jesse Ventura. This was after Kyle reported Ventura uttered a phrase that the Navy SEALs "deserve to lose a few."

Ventura countered that what Kyle wrote was untrue. He also had to prove actual malice in order to win the judgment.

In a twist of fate, Kyle was killed at a Texas gun range, and his widow controlled the proceeds from the book's royalties and movie rights, which were deemed to be upwards of $15 million.

Kyle proclaimed Ventura hated America and disparaged him to the point that it caused serious harm to the former Minnesota governor and professional wrestler's reputation and financially.

1.3 Woman arrested for alleged cyberbullying

A Pekin woman obtained a topless selfie photograph of another woman and posted it on Facebook[3]. She was charged with harassment by electronic communication, a misdemeanor, which comes with a two-year sentence.

1.4 Restaurant review gone bad

In 2012, Ottawa restaurant owner Marisol Simoes was convicted for her two-year online assault against Elayna Katz, who gave her establishment

2   "Jesse Ventura wins $1.8 million in defamation case over 'American Sniper' book," Syracuse.com, accessed November, 2014. www.syracuse.com/news/index.ssf/2014/07/jesse_ventura_defamation_american_sniper_book_chris_kyle.html
3   "Woman arrested for alleged cyberbullying," PekinTimes.com, accessed November, 2014. www.pekintimes.com/article/20140618/NEWS/140618977/10082/NEWS

a bad review[4]. She faced up to five years in prison for two counts of libel as she campaigned to humiliate the reviewer.

1.5 $20 million awarded in Internet libel case

Phillip Maurice "Marty" Hicks was hit with a default judgment in September 2011 when he disobeyed a summons to participate in discovery for an Internet defamation case against him. During the course of his cyber libel campaign against Revolutions Medical Corporation, it was deemed that Hicks intentionally obstructed a 2010 Department of Defense grant that would fund the distribution of its patented safety syringes to its HIV/AIDS Prevention Program. Revolutions Medical Corporation and its Chief Executive Officer Rondald Wheet were awarded $20 million[5].

1.6 Scientist awarded cyber libel damages

Pat Holley accused archeologist Cheryl Ross of being a grave robber and posted slanderous false accusations coupled with pictures said to be human remains on a public site and circulated emails for people to spread virally.

Holley was known to Dr. Ross through his wife, who Ross met while working on an Indian reserve. Holley blamed Ross for the breakup of his marriage. An Ontario court judge awarded Dr. Ross $125,000 in damages for publishing malicious, defamatory, and untrue comments.

1.7 *Sabbato v. Hardy*, Ohio Court Appeal, December 18, 2000

Hardy owned a website where users could post and read opinions. He was accused of participating in defamatory comments[6] against Sabbato. Ohio's lower court ruled immunity for Hardy under Section 230 of the Communications Decency Act. The appellate court reversed the decision.

1.8 *Varian v. Delfino and Day*, Santa Clara County, 2001

This was a case where two former employees spread over 14,000 messages to over 100 websites disparaging its former company Varian. A

---

4   "Online defamation cases often unrealistic for Canadians: Expert," GlobalNews.ca, accessed November, 2014.
    http://globalnews.ca/news/674540/online-defamation-cases-often-unrealistic-for-canadians-expert
5   "$20 Million Awarded in Internet Libel Case," MarketWired.com, accessed November, 2014.
    www.marketwired.com/press-release/20-million-awarded-in-internet-libel-case-1807422.htm
6   "US cases on cyber libel in message boards and forums," Burleson Consulting, accessed November, 2014.
    www.dba-oracle.com/internet_cyberlibel_usa_cases_message_boards_forums.htm

jury found Delfino and Day guilty of Internet libel. Varian was awarded $425,000.

1.9 Nouveau Riche International Model and Talent Management and TheDirty.com[7]

Employees told Nouveau Riche International Model and Talent Management CEO Rose Rosales about the nameless slanderous comments they found about her and the company on TheDirty.com.

The US gossip website does not vet any comments, pictures, or posts made on the site for untruths and defamation. Users hiding behind the cloak of anonymity accused the company was fraudulent and that Rosales didn't pay her models.

The Internet was a huge part of the company's identity. The website did not remove any of the posts as Rosales had asked. She knew that when people did a Google search, they would see these posts front and center, so the libel had a severe economic impact on her business. When a website is popular, it is harder to bury the posts.

Rosales could sue TheDirty.com for legal action, but that company's resources would likely be greater than the modeling company's. A favorable judgment doesn't guarantee the offending posts will be removed, as the third parties are immune. Instead, a removal notice was issued under the Digital Millennium Copyright Act, but was unlikely to be successful. Her only option would be to find the anonymous commenters and sue them directly.

1.10 Byong-Jon Kim v. Dongpo News, Kwang Ho Song, and John Doe

Kim sued Dongpo[8] to remove false, misleading, and defamatory statements in articles it had published. Not only did the judge award Kim $75,000, it ordered Dongpo to remove the content and restrained it from publishing further such statements.

Kim was successful in another judgment against the Korean Forum and received the same sum.

---

7   "Canadian Business Harmed by Online Defamation," KellyWarnerLaw.com, accessed November, 2014.
    http://kellywarnerlaw.com/canadian-defamation-thedirty-com
8   "Canadian Internet Defamation Rulings," McConchie Law Corporation, accessed November, 2014.
    www.libelandprivacy.com/cyberlibel_home.html

1.11 Teacher "powerless" to stop ex-girlfriend's cyberstalking

An ex-girlfriend has cost Lee David Clayworth his teaching career[9]. He dated Lee Ching Yan in Malaysia where he taught in 2010.

When they ended the relationship, Yan criminally entered Clayworth's apartment, hacked into his computer, then distributed terrible untruths, comments, and nude photos of him to his email contacts and on a number of social media sites. Her relentless cyberstalking and harassment stemmed over two and a half years.

Yan had to be sued in Malaysia, and while Yan was found guilty of defamation and ordered a judgment of $66,000, she continued to harass him. Meanwhile, he can't get the content removed from the search engines, so anyone trying to vet him will come across these defamatory posts.

1.12 Texas couple awarded $13 million in defamation case

Mark Lesher and his wife proved that some people can't hide anonymously behind the First Amendment and defame people[10]. The couple found themselves in a legal battle in 2009, when they were accused of sexual assault but acquitted in court. However, a website allowed the trial to continue when anonymous avatars spread horrible and vile comments about the couple in its discussion feed.

The Leshers sued the website, which was forced to hand over the Internet addresses of the commenters. It was soon discovered that computers used to write the defamatory comments were traced back to the Lesher's original accusers.

1.14 Jury awards $11.3M over defamatory Internet posts

Sometimes being right means more than the cost it takes to get there. When Sue Scheff sued Carey Bock[11] for calling her a crook, a fraud, and a con artist all over the Web, she knew Bock would not be able to pay any of the judgment and she was quite willing to pay all the court costs relating to the case.

---

9   "Teacher 'powerless' to stop ex-girlfriend's cyberstalking," CBC.ca, accessed November, 2014.
      www.cbc.ca/news/canada/british-columbia/teacher-powerless-to-stop-ex-girlfriend-s-cyberstalking-1.1314610
10 "Texas couple awarded $13 million in Web defamation case," Wfaa.com, accessed November, 2014.
      www.wfaa.com/story/local/2014/08/30/13868638
11 "Jury awards $11.3M over defamatory Internet posts," USAToday.com, accessed November, 2014.
      http://usatoday30.usatoday.com/news/nation/2006-10-10-internet-defamation-case_x.htm

Scheff even knew Bock, but she wanted to send a message for people to stop using the Internet to destroy each other.

2. Cyber Heroes

2.1 Lindsay Bottos

Artist turns cyberbullying messages into empowered art for women

Art student Lindsay Bottos, 21, created an artistic portfolio of selfies, embedded with cyberbully comments she had received[12] as an empowerment tool. This turned into empowered art for women to snub their nose at cyberbullying.

What did she do that engaged such anger from the cyber trolls? She didn't shave her armpits.

2.2 Bill Belsey

The cyber-address www.bullying.org is the world's most-visited and referenced website about bullying. It is also the first website formed that has addressed the issue of cyberbullying. Bill Belsey created the site and is considered a leading authority to talk about this issue.

Belsey instigated the annual National Bullying Awareness Week (www.bullyingawarenessweek.org) and formed the educational resource www.bullyingcourse.com, which provides online courses and webinars about bullying and cyberbullying.

Belsey has been honored many times over:

- Childnet International Award for Internet initiatives making the world a safer place for youth.

- Finalist for the Stockholm Challenge Award.

- The Nobel Prize of Information Technology.

- Winner of the Prime Minister's Award for Teaching Excellence in Science, Mathematics, and Technology.

- Recipient of the Royal Bank Fellowship from the Mathematics, Science, and Technology Group at Queen's University and the

  Roy C. Hill Fellowship for Innovations in Education from the Canadian Teacher's Federation.

---

12 "Artist Turns Awful Cyberbullying Messages Into A Way To Empower Women (Photos)," EliteDaily.com, accessed November, 2014. http://elitedaily.com/women/using-online-bullying-empower-women

- 2004 Cochrane Alberta's "Ambassador of the Year".

- Asked to offer his input into the United Nations International Research Study in Bangkok on Violence and Children in 2005.

- 2006 Canada's National Technology Innovations Award from The Learning Partnership. His "Change the World 101" presentation was given the Conference Award as the most outstanding work presented.

- 2006 Fellow of the World Technology Network in the Education category at a San Francisco's City Hall gala event where former US Vice President Al Gore was inducted as a Fellow.

- 2007 nomination for the YMCA Peace Medal.

- 2011 testimony about bullying and cyberbullying to the Human Rights Committee of the Canadian Senate.

- 2012 Queen Elizabeth II Diamond Jubilee Medal.

2.3 Jada

A 16-year-old girl is slut-shamed on social media[13] after she passed out from a drink she was handed at a party and then was raped[14]. She learned about the incident only after the photos went viral on social media. There were pictures of her passed out, both fully clothed on the bed and naked on the floor. The hashtag was #jadapose. People tweeted pictures of themselves in the same position with the hashtag.

The only reason she attended the party was because her friend knew the host. Of course her rapist has declared he didn't do it and his friends rallied behind him and continued to spread disparaging comments on the web with the #jadapose hashtag.

Jada took back the Internet, posting her own picture of her standing with her fist raised up with the hashtags: #IAmJada #JadaCounter-Pose.

2.4 Mean Tweets on Jimmy Kimmel Live

When celebrities read mean Tweets about themselves[15], it not only helps them regain their power, it shows the authors for who they are.

13 "Disgusting Hashtag Attacking Teen Rape Victim Goes Viral," Tytnetwork.com, accessed November, 2014. www.tytnetwork.com/2014/07/10/disgusting-hashtag-attacking-teen-rape-victim-goes-viral
14 "Teen 'Rape Victim', Jada, Bravely Fights Back Against Internet Trolls And Victim Blaming," HuffingtonPost. co.uk, accessed November, 2014. www.huffingtonpost.co.uk/2014/07/17/jadapose-american-girl-rape-victim-viral-_n_5594899.html
15 "'Mean Tweets' on 'Jimmy Kimmel Live': Which celebrities asked for meaner tweets?," InsideTV.ew.com, accessed November, 2014. http://insidetv.ew.com/2014/06/17/jimmy-kimmel-live-celebrities-read-mean-tweets

When Kimmel noticed what was being said about him, he also realized he was not the only one, and that offered him a bit of comfort.

Since the segment has gained attention, some have asked to come on his show and read their tweets. It shows that celebrities are human, not this untouchable ego-driven entity that is an easy target for bullies.

2.5 Dan Rice and David Liebensohn

It's called Censorgram and it is mobile phone app created by two Oklahoman cousins[16]. While the app has yet to be patent-approved, its design is to automatically delete comments from a user's images or videos on Instagram.

Founders Dan Rice and David Liebensohn have experienced cyberbullying firsthand with one of their businesses and one of their daughters.

The app is available in both iTunes and Google Play Store and has a 4.4/5 review rating. People who like the app have said[17]:

- "I've been trying this app out on my own account ... thanks for such a great creation!"

- This user goes on to add that her kids are not old enough yet for a social media account, which is why she wanted to test it out on hers.

- "Best app ever! Great app for the family ... "

2.6 Sometimes just speaking out is an act of bravery

Jess was 22 and dating "Matt," but his ex-girlfriend "Jenna" took exception to the relationship and began to cyber-harass Jess[18]. Jenna made up fake Facebook profiles and spread hateful comments about both Jess and Matt. Her lies caused some of Jess's connections to harass her and troll her social media feeds about the awful things she was alleged to have done.

Jess blocked as many of her bullies as she could and at the time had difficulty in blocking these people on Twitter.

Her mother counseled her to report the harassment to the police, but the officer who met with her suggested she should just get over

---

16 "Oklahoman cousins develop anti cyber-bullying app," Koco.com, accessed November, 2014.
   www.koco.com/news/oklahoman-cousins-develop-anti-cyberbullying-app/26757098#!bFmgg9
17 "Censorgram," Google play, accessed November, 2014.
   https://play.google.com/store/apps/details?id=com.appsocial.censorgram&hl=en
18 "Jess has faced cyberbullying as an adult," Cybersmile.org, accessed November, 2014.
   www.cybersmile.org/blog/jess-has-faced-cyberbullying-as-an-adult

it and delete her accounts. Jess was not ready to end her relationships with family and friends who connected with her in social networks because of an insensitive policeman, who also suggested she contact Jenna and hash out their differences. It had only escalated the abuse and resulted in more people piling on in Jenna's favor.

The abuse spilled into the offline world, where Jenna's friends would accost Jess in public.

Jess's way of fighting back was to become a #cybersmiler and put herself out there for anyone else to share their story with her.

12

Take Back the Internet and Your Life

You have the power to rewrite your story

http://about.me/debbie.elicksen

While you can't appear to remove the hate posts against you, Diane Ojar-Ali reminds us, "It's someone's opinion. The people who know you, know you."

Nobody seems to be policing the Internet with respect to cyberbullying and finding help to deal with it can be a daunting task.

Ojar-Ali admits, "It also seems like it is a full-time job that you have to keep hunting and looking. It's sad when you have a passion about something, and when you go out to do it, you have to watch your back."

You can't live in fear. Everyone makes mistakes. Everyone has a skeleton in the closet. If a bully decides to seize the opportunity to publish your sins and kick you when you're down, the good news is that with today's digital highway, attention spans are short.

People need to forgive themselves first.

Do not let other people's criticism define who you are. The bully wants attention and to be validated. You may have to rebuild your business. It happens. Even if he or she is still in pursuit of you, it's time to take ownership of what you do and be true to yourself.

We have to cut ourselves a little slack. Besides, digital is only the medium. It's not the mindset.

1. Drown the Internet with Good Content

You are now going to be a search engine optimizer; the SEO of your digital content. This is how you can use the Internet for good and try to bury the troll's posts at the same time.

Note that your cyberbully may be using the same content to ensure his or her vile content stays current. Even so, doing these steps will ensure his/her voice is not the only voice online about you.

Figure out what keywords your bully is focusing on. Write blog posts and post videos geared around those keywords. Make sure you use those keywords in all of your SEO efforts.

First and foremost, if you don't have one already, set up a Google+ profile. You really need this for Google to play nice with your SEO efforts. Because Google owns the universe, it will push your content (if your content isn't spam and useless dribble) ahead of others who are not in Google+. Unfair, yes, but it is Google's universe. Deal with it. Try and post something at the very minimum, once a week. Use hashtags to describe what is in the content. For example, this book would be #internettrolls #cyberbully #cyberbullying #businesscyberbullying #bully

#howtofightbackfromacyberattack #debbieelicksen #selfcounselpress. Don't piss Google off by using a hashtag that doesn't apply to the content. That will not win you favor in the rankings.

Make your profile as detailed as you would if you were sending a resume to Disney to be its next CEO. Include all your links to other sites, blogs, and pretty much everything that you have created online. Let your Google+ profile be the Internet wormhole where all of your online content can be sucked into one place.

If you don't have any other sites to link to online, get busy and create some. This is how marketing works today, anyway. You need to learn this. (I just happened to have another book through Self-Counsel Press that can help you with this.)

Be in the key social media sites, like Facebook, Twitter, and LinkedIn. If you cater to a younger audience, get on Tumblr and Instagram, too. If you like taking pictures, get yourself a Flickr account. Your being in all of these sites adds another search result in your Google feed. Some of the posts will show up in Google individually, mostly from Google, blogs, Flickr, YouTube, and Twitter. Facebook and Google haven't married yet and are still playing hard to get with each other, so your individual posts won't show up in the search engine.

1.1 What is good content?

Good content is anything positive. It isn't arguing politics, saying how terrible shape the world is in, or any negative, toxic banter that is Debbie Downer material. (http://www.urbandictionary.com/define.php?term=Debbie+Downer)

Be the beacon of light that everyone is looking for. Be a good digital citizen. If you have people troll your feeds and post crap, delete it. YOU control your social media and your content.

Be an educator. Now that you've gone through this, maybe you can help someone else who is too afraid to talk about it and needs help. Offer the information in a positive and constructional way. For example, when it was my turn to fight back, my web co-hosting partner Cynthia K. Seymour suggested I write numerous blog posts about cyberbullying that would help others through the process. She rattled off a list of topics that could become individual blog entries, which could then be republished with additional unique content and in different formats at least 13 different times on numerous platforms.

Here is that list. You can do the same with any experience with which you want to create good Internet content. Notice the slight variations on a similar angle. This can be a guide on how to stretch your topic angle. In fact, I may use some of these when I'm ready.

1. Here are the steps I took to stop cyberbullying.

2. Cyberbullying experts.

3. Reporting cyberbullying.

4. A topic of research.

5. How I went against my own cyberbully.

6. How to document a case against cyberbullying.

7. What to do if you get cyberbullied.

8. What to do about cyberbullying.

9. How to deal with a cyberbully.

10. How to defend your honor online.

11. Protect your reputation against cyberbully.

12. What your business can do against a cyberbully.

13. Ten tips for handling cyberbullies.

14. How to fire-bolt your cyberbully.

15. Fighting fire with fire against your cyberbully.

16. Keyboard cowards: Top ten cyberbullies.

17. Heroes against cyberbullies.

18. Top ten Twitterers fighting cyberbullies.

19. Celebrities facing cyberbullies.

20. Top ten lawyers against cyberbullying.

21. Top ten legal cases re: cyberbullying.

22. When does a trashy post turn into cyberbullying?

23. Experts teaching about cyberbullying.

24. Organizations dealing with cyberbullying.

25. Celebrities standing up against cyberbullies.

26. What is cyberbullying?

27. Terminology: libel; civil versus criminal; defamation; unlawfully accusing of a crime.

28. Resources: Cease and desist letter template.

29. How to document using screenshots.

30. Trademark/copyright.

31. Sticking your head in the sand.

32. Phases of depression.

33. Emotional impact of cyberbullying.

34. You are not the victim.

35. Knowing who your real friends are.

36. How to protect yourself.

37. How to talk to the police.

38. Combat tactics.

39. Document your case.

40. Cyberbullying isn't just a student issue.

41. Social media settings (prevention).

42. Turn off your geo tags.

2. Pay or Do-It-Yourself SEO

There are number of reputation management services you can use to help bury negative content online. Some of the personal concierge services may run you anywhere from $3,000 to $5,000 to $20,000. It really depends on the level of service you require and the company fee schedule.

If you don't have the money to banter around, try a site like http://brandyourself.com. Set up a profile and link it to all your networks. The site culls the Internet and evaluates positive and negative links, and also gets you to confirm them. It has a free version where you have limited management, and it has a fee-service, where you can submit unlimited links and provide a better option for getting content buried.

Typically it takes about six months to a year for negative content to get buried.

3. Taking Back Your Life: Healing from the Inside Out

When people hurt you over and over, think of them like sand paper; They may scratch and hurt you a bit, but in the end, you end up polished and they end up useless.

— CHRIS COLFER

Getting your digital footprint back in order is one thing, but what about regaining your inner balance?

Your cyberbully has assaulted you: mind and soul. You can't just shrug it under the carpet and expect the pain to go away. It is real pain. You deserve to be free mentally, so you can soar and rebuild your house of self-respect.

Annette Stanwick is one of the most amazing people you could ever meet. She exudes light. That hasn't always been the case. Her brother was murdered and she went through a lot of deep and unending pain. She had some very dark thoughts. She eventually found her way through it, thanks to her faith, and remarkably, she forgave her brother's killer publicly, in the courtroom. She was so moved by the experience, she wrote *Forgiveness: The Mystery and Miracle* to help others transform through pain.

That wasn't Stanwick's only extreme life challenge. She escaped an attempted abduction, she experienced being shot, and she survived a nearly fatal head-on collision that put her in the hospital for several months. She is a renowned speaker and facilitator and she tells people what they need to hear.

"The journey to healing can only start when we acknowledge we've been hurt. When we can acknowledge that we are suffering some pain. When we can acknowledge that we are angry, that we are frustrated, that we are hurting so deeply, when we're resentful, bitter — all of that plethora of negative emotions. We can heal from things when we acknowledge them, but if we can't acknowledge them, it is very difficult to heal."

Something that is painful for you may not be painful for me and the other way around. We all have individual trigger points and perspectives. But the bottom line is: Pain is pain. When we've been hurt, it creates a wound. That wound needs to heal. Some of those wounds can be very deep.

Stanwick describes a situation where a woman was in business with a friend. Everything seemed to be going all right, so she thought. They had borrowed a lot of money, too. Then suddenly, he just disappeared on her. He had embezzled thousands. They also had no contract because they were friends. There was nothing to prove he was in business with her, so she was left holding the bag for the loans he left her with.

"She was angry. She was so angry that she wanted to kill him. She even found somebody who was willing to do that. She paid a portion of the money. Then she heard me speak, and it changed her mind. If she would have had this guy killed, she would have ended up in prison herself, and the wounds, the hurt, the resentment, and the bitterness would just go on."

Anyone who has gone through having a reputation dragged through the mud by a cyberbully can certainly understand this woman wanting the source of her pain to be wiped off the face of the earth. But lashing out tends to draw that toxic energy right back at us. Instead, Stanwick has a plan to guide people through their journey to inner healing.

It's the Five Step Freedom Formula:

1. **Face the issues.** When we've been hurt, we need to face what the issues are. There may be several issues that are layered on top of each other. Name all of them, for example: Have I been embezzled? Has my reputation been tarnished? Have I lost friends? Have I lost money? Have I lost reputation? Have I lost business?

2. **Feel the pain.** Stanwick knew another businesswoman who had one of her trusted and valued employees abscond with her entire database. She didn't have the safeguards or policies in place to avoid such an event, was too trusting, and ultimately let this person have access to anything and everything. For this woman, the pain was the self-loathing. She had been betrayed. The self-loathing was enormous. Here she was this entrepreneur with a multi-million-dollar cyber business and she learned she didn't

have the right things in place to prevent this from happening. She hated herself. She laid all the blame on herself and experienced huge guilt and shame. She was supposed to be a role model. She thought she was branded, that she was stupid.

"Feeling the pain of the situation is really important. Write down and list all the types of pain, and feel them. What does it feel like to have so much guilt, to feel so much shame? To think that the whole world is going to be looking at you and thinking, you're a fraud because you didn't even take care of your own house."

Depression can waft in and lead to suicidal feelings. Look at what I've done. Look at my failings. I am a huge failure. Or you could want to take the other person out — to kill them, for real. Know that anger towards the inside leads to depression, self-loathing, and low self-esteem.

The anger doesn't do us any good. Instead, talk about it. Acknowledge the anger, the loss, the grief, and the deep resentment. The list can go on and on, but it's important to make the list. When we make the list, we are facing the pain.

3. **Make positive choices.** We may not be able to control the things that happen to us, but we always have a choice in how we respond. Reach out to someone and talk about it. Go to seminars. Do some reading. For the person who has been cyberbullied, do some research. Reach out to other people who have been through a similar experience.

Get some help. Go to a lawyer, have some coaching. Educate yourself. Search answers on the Internet. Take control of those things you can take control of. But do not to bash your bully. That plays right into their pathology. Disengage from them. Be as positive as possible.

We know who we are inside. When an individual has been maligned us, we can't take it personally, but it is hard not to.

4. **Let go of the hurt.** "After my brother was murdered," Stanwick conveys, "I think the choices I made were so powerful. This goes back to the third step. I made the choice I wanted to be happy again. I did not want to be consumed. I wanted to grow. Make the choice to not be consumed by it. You are much more valuable than what that person is saying."

If you can make the choice to be happy again, in spite of what has happened, that is one step in rising above. Healing is about rising above what has happened. We can't change what has happened. We can only learn to let go of it.

Stanwick articulates, "The title of my seminar is 'Letting Go and Living Free.' I get someone up on the platform with me and I have them imagine that I am the person they are angry with. Then I have a chain that I wrap around them and I wrap around me. They are actually chained to me, but they have both ends of the chain in their hands. They have control. Everywhere they go across the platform, they take me along. When I go somewhere (as someone who has bullied them or hurt them), they follow me, because they've chained themselves to me. I've been talking to them about letting go. Let go of that person. Let go. Then I'd say, 'What do you need to do?' They say, 'Well, I need to let go.' Me: 'Okay, so what do you need to do?' Them: 'I guess I need to drop the chain.' Me: 'So?' Then the lights come on (in his/or her head) and they let go of the chain. It drops and they can hardly believe it - the difference. They are no longer attached or chained to that person who has hurt them."

When you write everything out, if you rip it up, burn it, or read it to someone else, it is a symbolic gesture.

Letting go is actually the forgiveness piece. Although, people don't like the term "forgive." They think it means they condone what has happened. Forgiveness is not condoning. Wrong will always be wrong.

When people are besmirched on the Internet, when reputations are destroyed, that is wrong. That will always be wrong. We could look more closely at that person, and ask, what is it about them that they had the need to besmirch someone else, to tarnish their reputation, to take their business down, and hurt them? They're likely hurting and afraid themselves. They want to bring other people down to their level — just like when you want to hire the hitman — you want to bring them down and make them hurt as much as they hurt you.

Hurt and the pain destroys us on the inside. Okay, it's happened. Now what am I going to do about it? How will I recover? Start by refusing to allow that bully to control you. Refuse to allow whatever happened to be the consuming force in your life. Let go of that and move forward.

Stanwick can tell you first-hand, "The power from letting go is so phenomenal. Then we can feel the freedom."

5. **Feel the freedom.** We often have to give ourselves permission to feel the freedom. For some reason, we think we shouldn't feel relief or release. Realize the bully is a misguided person. He has psychiatric problems. He is deeply wounded and is trying to hurt you and others because he's been hurt badly. Stanwick suggests that if we could have compassion for him, if we really knew his story but that could take years and a lifetime to come to a point of empathy, if ever.

Stanwick herself has been the target of a cyberbully. "I was maligned by an individual. He took exception to something I had said on the Internet, which was an inspirational quote. He was a Christian. He couldn't understand how I, as a Christian, could put that particular image on Facebook. He thought it represented some other faith background. He made some really derogatory comments. I said Christianity doesn't have a corner on the market of having really inspirational thought. He took it to a higher level in the Christian world.

"I blocked him, number one, from even looking at my Facebook. He did some deep searching and took screenshots of things that I had shared from other sources that he thought was absolutely wrong for me to do — that I was perhaps dabbling in some other faith groups. That was defamation. Because of where he took that — he took it to a really high organization where my husband was pastoring. He took it to the national board, and they wrote a letter to me saying I was approaching blah, blah, blah. It made me laugh at how they had interpreted this."

Stanwick accepted quotations from all kinds of sources. If they were inspirational and meaningful, she would share them. Her philosophy was, if she wanted people to listen to her, she would have to be willing to share other people's words.

"I wrote a letter back. I told them, that by taking it to this board, that it really was defamation of character. I could tell that they were really worried that I was going to take legal action.

I've chosen not to do anything legally. It would do no good. It would consume me to figure out what it was they're looking at, to try and defend myself. I didn't have that kind of energy, and what would I gain in the long run?"

She and her husband chose to not take legal action, but they did talk with a lawyer about it. He did say she had a case, but litigation would a long time, and it would have taken a lot of money. She would have had to use an extraordinary amount of time and energy to follow through.

"When I wrote back the letter, someone said he brought in a whole stack of evidence. We never did see what he had. At one point, he even said, you may even have a bit of demon possession. It was so crazy on how this all happened. I let it go. It's a story. I had to go through the five steps. The facts are there. It was hurtful at the time. I was astonished, but I did go through the five steps."

If we are bullied, we're the only ones who can let it go.

4. What If We're the Bully and We Don't Even Know It?

There are times we act like bullies and don't realize it. Annette Stanwick has had this experience, too.

"I spoke (to some schools) during anti-bullying week, and started out with asking them the question: 'Would you believe that I'm a bully?' I didn't know I was a bully until I was 40 years old.

"One of my brothers took me to my hometown cemetery. We had been there to visit our father's grave site. Then we walked through the cemetery and saw all the names we recognized and came to this one name, and it was Anita. Below the name, it said 'Here lies lonely Anita.' I said to my brother, 'What happened to Anita? She was in my class.' He said she committed suicide.

"Anita had lived in a junkyard or right next to a junkyard and she was in my class. We used to play tag in school. When we caught somebody, we'd say, 'You have Anita's fleas.' We called her Junkyard Anita. She would hide around the side of the school. When I saw that on her tombstone, I wept. I realized I was part of her pain. I wasn't the instigator of it but I went along with it. I participated in it. I saw her brother at an event and I went up to him and apologized. I told him what I did and that I was so sorry for how I had treated his sister. He thanked me."

When we know better, we do better. A lot of times we see behaviors in others that mirror some of the behaviors in us. At least, now that we are armed with the knowledge of what bullying is and the pain it causes, we can catch ourselves if we find that we are doing something out of spite.

Stanwick concludes that the one thing we can do with the five steps is to forgive ourselves.

It's hard to forgive ourselves because we believe we don't deserve to be forgiven. Apology is a very important part of self-forgiveness, even if it is in our prayers.

5. Step into the Light and Create Your Future

Thushyanthan Amirthelingam is an ontological coach who uses the foundational tenets of nonviolent communications, a communication process founded by Marshall Rosenberg. (http://en.wikipedia.org/wiki/Marshall_Rosenberg) Ontological coaching taps into a person's inner awareness and potential for developing new ways of seeing life. Nonviolence principles involve the natural state of compassion when no violence is present in the heart. (http://www.cnvc.org/)

When you internalize the bullying, you allow someone else to control your awareness. By learning to take control of your awareness, then you can come from a space of choice.

Amirthelingam affirms that nonviolent communication doesn't always refer to violence towards other people. It also addresses the scenario when we are very critical of ourselves. Nonviolence is both about externally and internally.

Rosenberg has a four-step process to separate the observation from the evaluation. Amirthelingam describes it as follows.

"Behind our eyes is an observer. An observer has a belief structure, and based on that belief structure, you get particular actions and results. Instead of going back and changing actions to get different results, we go back further and change that observer.

"Linguistically through the language that runs in our head, we move away from the opinions and the assessments, and come at it as an observer. What this requires is an understanding of your own emotions."

For example, if we look at anger as a spectrum that can lead to violence, for some people, it might mean smashing pots; for another it might mean raising their voice 10 decibels; for another it could be breathing hard and clenching fists. Where one person exhibits anger by breaking dishes, another person might see that as rage, and another might look upon that as irritation. These are three different words to describe a spectrum.

"So you've been bullied, now what?" throws out Amirthelingam. "We have already been taught that we shouldn't get angry. Because if we get angry, we're bad people. The reactions we have, the emotions we feel are picked upon when we feel there has been an injustice done to us. We respond by getting angry, and that's an emotion. So you work through the emotions and self-talk, angry, not right to get angry, bad for being angry, I was bad, so I was bullied."

For the observer to increase his or her vocabulary, it might mean going to a dictionary or thesaurus, and look at the entomology of a word like "anger."

We emote when our needs are missing. Amirthelingam contends that the process of emotion is natural. There is also a physiological component.

"Some people hunch when they are angry. We embody these emotions. We embody the language of emotions and thoughts."

Maslow's Hierarchy of Needs puts more weight on physical elements instead of the real deep interconnectedness that we deeply require as human beings. The list for internal connection is three times larger than the need for the physical.

We need to be accepted. We have a need to belong, to feel appreciation for ourselves, a sense of community, to be included, loved, safe, secure, and stable. Our emotion comes out when these needs are not met, and even when they are. Amirthelingam observes that one individual does not have to meet them.

"I've noticed when individuals move from the sense of ownership to responsibility, that they are responsible for their own emotions and actions, the energy they exude, most people might assess as being positive.

"You can go the legal route. You can fight back. Anger is emoting a sense that an injustice has been done to you. How you deal with injustice is up to that individual. Do they want a third party arbitrator? Does the law require this? Is the time and effort required greater than the time and effort it would take to rebuild?"

Amirthelingam comes from a Hindu perspective, where the belief is that things happen for a reason. One of the key things about non-violence is to do no harm in thought, word, and deed.

"There is a lesson to be learned. In some cases, the consequences of the bullying are tragic. Can you as an individual move past that into a space of acceptance of the facts? Without judgment?"

Each party in an event has their own assessments, linguistics, and emotions. Can you move the awareness from inside to outside and look at it without judgment? Once you do that, then you might be able to move into a space of forgiveness. Forgiveness does not mean forgetfulness. Forgiveness is the result for seeing the situation for what it is, for gathering that lesson, and committing to not relearn that lesson.

The emotion of gratitude is the story we tell ourselves is that life is a gift. Thankfulness is an acknowledgment of an exchange.

Creating a culture of awareness takes time.

> *Because I was surrounded by so much negativity at some point that it took me going back and doing stand-up to realize, you know, people really like me.*
>
> — DAVE CHAPPELLE

Conclusion

Today I choose life. Every morning when I wake up I can choose joy, happiness, negativity, pain ... To feel the freedom that comes from being able to continue to make mistakes and choices — today I choose to feel life, not to deny my humanity but embrace it.

— Kevyn Aucoin

Actress Gwyneth Paltrow spoke about the anonymity of the Internet at the Re/Code's Code Conference in 2014. She conveyed that being anonymous seems to allow trolls the liberty to objectify and dehumanize others[1], and compares them with the "scabs from your high school wounds being ripped off on a daily basis."

Public figures are especially fair game. Even though it comes with the territory, she admitted the firsthand devastating effects Internet trolls have had on her life, and has witnessed the toll it has taken on her high profile friends. When you post an innocent photograph on a social network and a commenter expresses a desire to rape and disembowel you, celebrity or not, it's going to affect you personally.

---

1   "Gwyneth Paltrow Calls Media Trolls 'Test of Our Emotional Evolution,'" NBCNews.com, accessed November, 2014. www.nbcnews.com/tech/social-media/gwyneth-paltrow-calls-internet-trolls-test-our-emotional-evolution-n115966

Even if you realize the comments are not really about you, but about the psyche of the individual posting the vile comments, it doesn't make seeing the posts any easier. It hurts, even if your self-esteem is high. The individuals with a low sense of self-worth might internalize it to the point of believing they are not worthy. Then when the Internet trolls feed on the post and escalate the online assault, the internalization might eat away at that person so much that they feel the only way to end the pain is to kill themselves.

During her talk, Paltrow left her audience with something to think about when she pronounced, "Perhaps the Internet has been brought to us as a test of our own emotional evolution."

Ultimately, even if we don't have control over what other people say about us publicly and privately, we do have control over our own mouse. We can click to read the terrible news or continue to look at the mean things people have to say. Or we can choose to hide the ugly images and comments from our online experience, and instead focus on the good side of the Internet.

Sara Hawkins adds, "Do stuff to get the positive community mobilized to squash the negativity. The average small business doesn't have the resources. Many of the people aren't savvy enough either, and they start getting very defensive because it is very personal. Then you start doing the things you really shouldn't do, which is deleting the comment, and just willy-nilly blocking people."

To add to what Hawkins said about blocking people, yes, you do block your tormenters after you've taken the screenshots for your Excrement file. But there are others in your online community who may have had a lapse in judgment and posted something that might be construed as pushing the envelope of hate. You can delete the comment, but keep the person.

I have a few people who sometimes add what I might think is a Debbie Downer comment to an otherwise positive feed. If it really takes away from the intention of my post, I might delete the comment. But if it is something that won't necessarily irritate everyone, then I'll leave it up. Most times, everyone else will ignore it. But there are times when a comment like that engages a meaningful discussion, and that's okay. I have had people I removed, not many, from my community because all they brought to the table was negativity and toxicity. I get to choose because it is my community.

When people complain about the quality of their feeds and how their community only offers non-valuable communications, I say get better friends. There are a ton of people out there, whether you currently know them or not, who bring extreme value to your Internet experience. I can't count how many Facebook friends I have, who I didn't know or who were not connected to anyone in my circles, who I allowed in and who ended up being better friends than some of the people I knew well outside of the Internet.

When you have your name trashed in Google, you will be surprised to see which friends stay and which ones unfriend you because they a) believe the post or b) they don't believe the post, but they think being associated with you might hurt them with their own connections.

Businesses do suffer and often at the hand of a competitor.

Yngve Hauge has walked 500 kilometers in four and a half weeks to create awareness about bullying. During the journey, he took pictures of the beauty of the world around him and shared them on social media. His website is a country-wide anti-bullying resource for Norwegians. He has a team of people to help with blog posts and educational content.

"Most people have some experience with bullying," Hauge has discovered. "You can't force someone to be friends. You can only share the solution, not the problem. Respect is the solution."

We all have the choice, whether we are the target of a bully or not, to bring the world down and make it feel our pain, or lift it up to be part of the solution. What a powerful statement to our cyberbully. We show them they can't control us based on what they have to say about us, and instead, we use love and respect to elevate the Internet. If everyone jumped on the positive train, then it will be the cyberbullies of the world that will be left alone in their own dark underworld of hate.

Fight back with love, and visit me at www.businesscyberbullying.com; I'd like to hear from you.

I have decided to stick with love. Hate is too great a burden to bear.

— Martin Luther King, Jr.